WRITING INSIGHTS

DISCOVERING THE KEYS TO STRUCTURE AND CONTENT

Revised Printing

PAUL AAMOT

EDITED BY GREGG AAMOT

Kendall Hunt
publishing company

Also by Paul Aamot:

Understanding English Grammar (1980)
Left-Right Confusion (1990)

Also by Gregg Aamot:

The New Minnesotans: Stories of Immigrants and Refugees (2006)

Cover image © Shutterstock.com

www.kendallhunt.com
Send all inquiries to:
4050 Westmark Drive
Dubuque, IA 52004-1840

Copyright © 2014 by Gregg Aamot

ISBN: 978-1-4652-9300-8
Revised Printing 2015, 2016, 2017

Published in the United States of America

DEDICATION

I happily and enthusiastically dedicate this work to my son, Gregg, who writes for The Associated Press. He credits his success as a professional writer to his having had a college freshman English teacher who used this book in her writing units. He insists that having been guided through *Writing Insights* by this teacher enabled him to enter a writing career without a bachelor's degree in journalism.

He has noted often that this book's new approach enabled him to acquire the "sentence sense" that professional writers need to write with confidence—the unerring sense of subordination and parallelism that handbooks, writing guides, readers, grammar texts, etc., do not provide.

His very positive experience with this book has encouraged me to seek further publication of this work and to promote its use in senior high and college writing courses. For this encouragement, I am extremely grateful!

About the Author

Paul Aamot was an English teacher for 35 years—13 years in senior high schools and 22 years in a small college. During that time he taught many writing classes. Most of the writing texts that were available did not seem to be very helpful. Most of them were writing handbooks, writing guides, grammar texts, readers, etc. that did not seem to address directly and clearly many of the problems students confronted as writers.

Directions and requirements for punctuation, for instance, were scattered throughout hundreds of pages in guides and handbooks. Many punctuation requirements were presented in almost incomprehensible grammatical directives, such as "place commas around all non-restrictive participle phrases" or "use commas after introductory adverb clauses."

Using these grammatical terms often seemed intimidating to students, so Mr. Aamot began creating handouts that made punctuation and other aspects of writing more understandable to students. These handouts ultimately resulted in this text, *Writing Insights*, which enables students to examine and identify the structure of every sentence they write, just as professional writers do. It also helps them sense the theses in what they read and write and better understand how writers defend those theses.

Editor's Note

A version of *Writing Insights* was first published as a textbook called *The Secrets of Writing* nearly three decades ago, yet it remains a singularly unique tool in the teaching of writing.

When I became a college teacher after many years in daily journalism, I adopted the book for use in both my English and journalism courses—mainly because I had used it as a college student and remembered how it had helped me master sentence structure and punctuation and better understand the creation and defense of theses. Many of my students have now had a similar experience, finding that the book greatly simplifies and clarifies what is often an intimidating task: learning to write acceptably.

Most colleges and universities require students to take two sections of English composition—one devoted to short expository writing and the other to research paper writing. *Writing Insights* can be used for both. As a rule of thumb, the first half of the text deals with sentence structure and the development of short papers while the second half delves into the more detailed work required for research paper writing.

This edition of *Writing Insights* contains updated exercises, practice tests and writing samples—presented in a fresh design for a new generation of students. The concepts and ideas behind this new approach to writing, however, have not changed and remain the sole work of the author.

Gregg Aamot
May 2014

A Note to Teachers and Students

This book, *Writing Insights*, is likely very different from the writing books you have used in the past and from other available writing texts. It uses a completely different approach to the teaching of writing. It should be used primarily as a supplemental writing text in writing classes for seniors in high school and for freshman English writing courses in college. For most students, these classes will be the last shots they will have at learning what they need to know about writing to write acceptably and confidently in their college classes and in their careers.

Many available writing texts bear titles like "A Writing Handbook," "A Guide to Writing," "A Reader," "A Grammar Guide," etc. Most are like dictionaries or reference books in which students can look up standards of usage in punctuation, grammar and sundry other elements of writing. But there seem to be no comprehensive writing texts that identify major aspects of writing that professional writers ultimately must understand and master to have their work accepted by the writing industry.

Do students need to reach that level? Most emphatically, yes! High school teachers and college professors constantly read material by professional writers. Guess what level they expect in student papers.

Writing Insights does not, of course, cover all aspects of writing, but it does zero in on several major aspects of writing skills that students must acquire to write acceptably and confidently. Professional writers must ultimately acquire "sentence sense"—a very keen understanding of sentence structure. They need this "sentence sense" to punctuate acceptably—to comply with punctuation practices that have evolved over the last century or so. Students need this "sentence sense," as well, but many do not have it by the time they finish high school, or even college.

Writing Insights is an effort to fill that very important gap in the teaching of writing. It does so mainly through exercises that help students recognize the structure of sentences by becoming aware of subordination and parallelism in sentences written by professionals. Writing is basically talk written down. In talking, subordination and parallelism do not pose problems. These aspects are taken care of in speech through inflections, emphasis, etc. and pose no problems, especially not for students who have been using the language since they were three years old and generally use the language very well. But in writing, subordination and parallelism require certain punctuation practices that we do not have to worry about when we speak. And that can be very intimidating for students who have been admonished to "use commas around all non-restrictive participle phrases" and to "set off all introductory adverb clauses with a comma" and been exposed to countless other incomprehensible and needlessly complicated directives.

Writing Insights helps students sense the structure of sentences in terms of a main part, plus sub-ordinate elements—basically introductions, interruptions and extensions that are set off from the main part of the sentence with commas, colons and dashes. Parallelism is handled by keeping elements that are doubled, tripled or more alike in structure and separated by commas and semi-colons in segments called compounds and series. This is what professional writers must become conscious of to punctuate acceptably and students deserve to learn as much.

Most students are good readers and when they read, they are primarily interested in "what does it say?"—as, of course, they should be. But when they write, students must—as professional writers do—tear themselves away from "what does it say?"—from content—to examine carefully the structure of the sentences they have written. To do that, students must somehow acquire the "sentence sense" that all professional writers and editors seem to have and that students generally—through no fault of their own—do not have. Students must somehow become sensitive to the main parts of each sentence they write and read. They must become skillful about recognizing the subordination and parallelism in many sentences—the introductions, interruptions, exten-sions, compounds and series—and must punctuate these elements acceptably, conforming to punctuation practices that have evolved in the writing industry. Insofar as sentence structure and punctuation is concerned, both student and professional writers must be conformists. *Writing Insights* can help students master this very important aspect of writing—sentence sense.

Writing Insights—in a long series of exercises—compels students to identify the structure of sentences written by professional writers. These opportunities for students to study—and ul-timately discover—the structure of sentences can result in a "behavior modification" that can prove to be invaluable to high school or college students who are concerned about being able to confidently meet any future writing assignment.

Students and adults who somehow learn, become aware of, the "sentence sense" that profes-sional writers have and use should not have trouble sensing the structure of sentences written by professionals. To do so, however, they must, momentarily at least, tear themselves away from the content—the meaning of the sentence—and concentrate strictly on its structure—the subordina-tion (introductions, interruptions and extensions) and the parallelism (compounds, series, etc.) that may be used in the sentence.

Here is a sentence followed by some graphics that suggest how some professional writers might observe the structure of sentences they have writ-ten in order to punctuate acceptably:

> In the Middle East, there are three countries—Saudi Arabia, Iran and Iraq—that have two extremely valuable nat-ural resources: vast reserves of oil and gas.

Without the "sentence sense" that a text like *Writing Insights* teaches, students will simply see words broken up by punctua-tion, something like this:

> XXXXXXXXXX, XXXXXXXXXXXXXXX—XXXXXXX, XXXXXXXX—XX XXXXXX XXXXXXXXXXXXXXXXXXXXXX: XXXXX XXXXXXXXXXXX.

They should, however, see something like this:

> *In the Middle East*, there are three countries—**Saudi Arabia, Iran and Iraq**—that have two extremely valuable natural resources: <u>vast reserves of oil and gas.</u>

For a student who has acquired "sentence sense," the different parts of the sentence—which in this work will be identified as **introductions**, **interruptions**, **extensions** and **main parts**—should come into sharp relief. (Note that the introduction is in italics, the interruption is in boldface and the extension is underlined while the main part is in normal typeface.)

A key to the sentence parts:
Introduction=*In the Middle East*
Main part=there are three countries that have two extremely valuable natural resources
Interruption=**Saudi Arabia, Iran and Iraq**
Extension=<u>vast reserves of oil and gas</u>

To further illustrate this idea, note the following six sentences—presented in bold face—that begin a review in the *New York Times Book Review* magazine.

(**Note:** If students can somehow acquire "sentence sense," they can read such sentences one at a time, momentarily ignore the content of each—as professional writers must do—and observe the "structure" of each sentence. They will be able to see a "structure" of each sentence somewhat like the description contained in the parentheses following each sentence.)

The writer of these six sentences understands the conventions of sentence structure that all professional writers adhere to. How a writer acquires such an un-

> **In the immediate aftermath of World War II, scholars, led by Hanna Arendt, routinely compared the Nazi and Soviet regimes, labeling them totalitarian.**
> (Students must ultimately be able to sense that the main part, the main subject-verb part, is "scholars routinely compared the Nazi and Soviet regimes" and that the other elements are an introduction, an interruption and an extension.)
>
> **Reacting against this school, a generation of revisionist historians has argued that it is unfair to tar the Soviet Union with the Nazi brush.**
> (A simple subordinate element, a short introduction, needs to be set off from the main part of the sentence with a comma.)
>
> **For all its failings, they claim, the Communist government was distinctly different from Nazi Germany and, they say, it brought positive benefits to the Soviet population.**
> (The main part is a compound sentence which is introduced with a short introduction set off with a comma. Two short interruptions are set off with commas—one in the introduction and one in the second part of the compound main part. The comma after "claim" ends both the introduction and the interruption.)

derstanding of structure is not easy to discern.

Some professional writers have worked one-on-one with an editor on some newspaper or magazine. Some journalism schools manage to duplicate such a one-on-one experience that would help students acquire "sentence sense." And certainly some non-professional writers—through a myriad of writing experiences—have a keen sense of structure. But, too often, even seemingly natural-born writers—who read voraciously and speak very well—are not confident about punctuation, an element they do not have to worry about when they speak.

Writers are conformists when it comes to structure, but they are non-conformists when it comes to con-

In the United States, and in much of the world, Nazism rightly has served the function of a moral absolute zero—a standard of evil—but the Soviet Union brought literacy, urbanization, hygiene and international standing to a country that in 1917 was overwhelmingly backward.

(Two phrases separated by a comma introduce the sentence, which has a compound main part separated by the conjunction "but." The sentence is somewhat complicated because of the abrupt interruption set off with dashes and the four parts of a series that need commas.)

The disintegration of the Soviet Union has finally freed historians from this sterile debate.

(There is no subordination or parallelism that needs punctuation. The sentence is a main part only.)

Beginning in 1992 with the publication of Alan Bullock's vast dual biography, "Hitler and Stalin: Parallel Lives," the comparative approach has returned in force.

(The short main part is introduced with a long subordinate element that contains an interruption—a title that is set off with commas. The comma after "Lives" serves both to end the interruption and to end the introduction.)

tent—their ideas, theses, explanations of relevance, etc. Students can read and write with greater ease and understanding if they understand conventional sentence structures—and conventional punctuation—used by professional writers.

SIMPLIFYING COMPLEXITY

To the right is a very complicated sentence about a biography of the writer Ernest Hemingway, *Ernest Hemingway: A Life Story.* Even such a long, complicated sentence can be understood by students if they sense its structure—its main part, its subordination and its parallelism.

> Highly anticipated at its release, this very readable biography of Ernest Hemingway by the Harvard scholar Carlos Baker, published eight years after the author's suicide at his home in Idaho, demystifies one of America's most famous writers—considered by one critic to be the most important author since Shakespeare—and gives readers a close look at a complicated artist who was a genius, a bore, a friend, an egotist and, above all, a masterful conveyor of 20th century disillusionment and perseverance.

Readers who have somehow acquired "sentence sense" will not be intimidated by such a sentence. They will note the main part (**"this very readable biography of Ernest Hemingway by the Harvard scholar Carlos Baker demystifies one of America's most famous writers and gives readers a close look at a complicated artist who was a genius, a bore, a friend, an egotist and a masterful conveyor of 20th century disillusionment and perseverance"**), will see the subordination that is set off with commas and dashes and will note the parallel elements, both compounds and series.

The exercises and examples in this supplemental writing text, *Writing Insights*, should help students become sensitive to this very important aspect of writing—"sentence structure."

CONTENT

Another very important aspect of writing that students must become keenly aware of is **content.** Perhaps the most important aspect of content has to do with the main point—the thesis, the conclusion, the judgment—that the writer has made about a subject, an issue, a controversy, or whatever. The other very important aspect of content is the defense of the thesis—the conclusion, the judgment. *Writing Insights* covers content primarily by helping students recognize the main idea of a piece of writing and the defense of the thesis. By observing many of the synonyms for judgments and many of the various forms of defense of judgments that writers can use, students can develop an awareness of the two most important aspects of content—main ideas and the defense of main ideas.

Writing Insights also deals with many of the usage problems writers must be aware of to write acceptably. Some usage problems involve faulty agreements, run-on sentences, distortions, etc., and are primarily related to structure. Other usage problems covered in *Writing Insights* involve faulty usage of words—such as wrong homonyms, grammatical errors, unidiomatic expressions, etc.

Students who diligently do the exercises and the assignments suggested in this book—and experience the resulting "behavior modification" as it relates to writing—should be able to write acceptably and confidently, both in college and in future career settings.

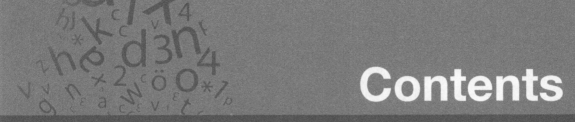

Contents

Insight #1:

Subordination

Most students are acquainted with the basic subject-verb elements in sentences. Even those who are not, however, will quickly learn, on the following pages, to distinguish the main parts of sentences from subordinate elements that need to be set off with punctuation. Professional writers know how to make this crucial distinction and students must, as well.

One important *insight*, then, that students of writing must acquire—insofar as **sentence structure** is concerned—is an awareness of **subordination**: the acceptable use of elements less important than the main part of the sentence.

INSIGHT #1: *Sentence Structure*: Sentences often have introductions, interruptions and extensions that must be set off from the main part of the sentence with commas, colons or dashes.

Unlike many student writers, professional writers seem to have a great deal of sentence sense. They know what the main part of each sentence is and they are aware of subordinate elements (less important parts that need to be set off with commas, colons and dashes).

To acquire the same sentence sense that professional writers have, students should study and work the following exercises.

Basically, the English sentence usually identifies a **subject** and some **action** (with a verb) that the subject does. The classic sentence in grade school—Boy hit Ball—identifies the subject—boy—and what he does—hit. The sentence also identifies the object of the action—ball.

Most English sentences perform these same three functions:

> *Zuckerberg created Facebook.*
> The *Democrats won* the *election.*
> The *investigation revealed corruption.*

A subtle variation of this Subject-Verb-Object sentence is another common type that reveals the condition of the subject or, as it is often stated, "the state of being" of the subject:

> *Zuckerberg was* the *founder.*
> *Democrats are* the *leaders.*
> The *investigation became intense.*

1

In these sentences, subjective complements follow the verbs instead of objects. The sentence have an SVC structure (subject-verb-complement). Then, too, some sentences do not have complements—neither objects nor subjective complements. They merely identify the subject and the action:

> *Zuckerberg acted.*
> The *Democrats won.*
> The *investigation faltered.*

Students **need not** recognize the difference between these basic types of sentences. (The only exception is the need to use the appropriate case: Boy hit *him*, but Boy is *he*. Students of writing, however, must be able to recognize this main part of every sentence they write and of every sentence they read.

MODIFIERS IN SENTENCES

Other elements in the sentence, which add detail or other information, are often what might be called **necessary modifiers**:

> *In 2005* **Zuckerberg** *ingeniously* **created Facebook.** *In 2012 the* **Democrats** *easily* **won** *the Presidential election.* *The Senate* **investigation revealed corruption** *in high places.*

For all practical purposes, these necessary modifiers can be considered *part of the main part* of the sentence. They are subordinate (modifying) elements, but they pose no problems for the writer other than some minor usage problems.

More important to the student writer are what might be called **extra modifiers** (often called *subordinate elements*). These elements, like necessary modifiers, also add detail or other information to sentences. However, they are generally set off from the main part of the sentence with commas, dashes or colons and, therefore, involve conventions (practices) of punctuation that every writer must be aware of.

EXTRA MODIFIERS: INTRODUCTIONS, INTERRUPTIONS AND EXTENSIONS

These extra modifiers are attached to the main part of sentences in three forms: **introductions**, **interruptions** and **extensions**. All are subordinate (less important) to the main part of the sentence, and their use is called subordination. In the following examples, notice how the extra modifiers are set off from the main part and necessary modifiers:

> *When he became restless with college,* **Zuckerberg,** *a coding prodigy like Bill Gates and Steve Jobs,* ingeniously **created Facebook,** *which has become the world's most popular social network.*

WRITING INSIGHTS: Discovering the Keys to Structure and Content

This sentence, like many English sentences, has a main part ("Zuckerberg ingeniously invented Facebook") plus three extra modifiers: an introduction, an interruption and an extension:

Introduction: *When he became restless with college*
Interruption: *a coding prodigy like Bill Gates and Steve Jobs*
Extension: *which has become the world's most popular social network*

Not all sentences, of course, have all three of these extra subordinate elements that need to be set off with punctuation. But most sentences seem to have at least one, and many have two or all three. The student writer, therefore, must be conscious of these main parts and subordinate elements to be able to punctuate acceptably. Also, several problems in usage can be solved by understanding subordination.

DISCOVERING THE EIGHT COMBINATIONS IN SENTENCES

To help students become aware of sentence structure, the following exercises emphasize the **eight combinations** of **main part** and **subordinate elements** that are possible in the construction of sentences. This is a key insight and students must know that there are not endless combinations that they need to be aware of; there are only eight. (There are no exceptions to this rule; those that seem to be are merely subtle forms and will be explained later.)

Here are the possible combinations:

A. Main Part only

B. Introduction and Main Part

C. Interruption and Main Part

D. Extension and Main Part

E. Introduction, Interruption and Main Part

F. Introduction, Extension and Main Part

G. Interruption, Extension and Main Part

H. Intro., Interruption, Extension and Main Part

From the exercises on the following pages, students should be able to acquire the necessary awareness of subordination needed to do most punctuation acceptably and to understand many common usage errors.

Before analyzing random sentences that might contain any one of the eight possible structures, it should be helpful to note some of the conventions (practices) that professional writers generally follow when they use these extra modifiers. These practices can perhaps be most easily explained by working first with sentences that have only a main part plus one subordinate element and then progressing to those with two or three.

Exercise #1:
Subordination

SUBORDINATION

A. Main Part only

B. Introduction and Main Part

C. Interruption and Main Part

D. Extension and Main Part

E. Introduction, Interruption and Main Part

F. Introduction, Extension and Main Part

G. Interruption, Extension and Main Part

H. Intro., Interruption, Extension and Main Part

Directions: Choose the letter above that most accurately identifies the structure of the following sentences:

Note: To clarify the various punctuation practices, the answers to many entries in these first exercises will be given and will also be explained. Also, the main parts of the sentences will be in all caps to help the student quickly distinguish main parts from subordinate elements.

First, the student should note that punctuation alone determines—in using this approach—whether an element is considered an extra modifier (subordinate element). Remember, our objective is to understand why writers punctuate as they do and, hopefully, to learn to punctuate acceptably.

```
1.   In 2004, MARK ZUCKERBERG
     CO-FOUNDED FACEBOOK.     1.   B

2.   IN 2004 MARK ZUCKERBERG
     CO-FOUNDED FACEBOOK.     2.   A

3.   MARK ZUCKERBERG, in 2004,
     CO-FOUNDED FACEBOOK.     3.   C

4.   MARK ZUCKERBERG CO-FOUNDED
     FACEBOOK, in 2004.       4.   D

5.   MARK ZUCKERBERG CO-FOUNDED
     FACEBOOK IN 2004.        5.   A
```

Usually such a short modifying element as "In 2004" is not set off with a comma, but writers may choose to do so—usually for emphasis. And when they do, they in a sense make it an introduction, an interruption or an extension—depending on where they place it in the sentence. That interpretation, at least, seems to help student writers understand what a professional writer does insofar as much punctuation is concerned.

As we will note, sometimes a writer has a choice whether to use a comma—whether to set off a subordinate element from the main part of the sentence. Short prepositions, for instance, are not ordinarily set off—except for clarity and emphasis:

In the first two, commas are needed for clarity; in the last one, the writer chose to use a comma for emphasis.

Using what you have learned from the examples above, provide answers for sentences 9 through 15:

Students often ask, "**How can one distinguish between main parts and subordinate elements?**" The answer is that main parts "can stand by themselves"; subordinate parts, in most cases, cannot. Examine any example in this book and you will note that the main part is grammatically a sentence. Introductions, interruptions and extensions may often have subjects and verbs, but the first word or the structure makes them subordinate—dependent on the main part. They cannot, generally, be made into sentences with a capital letter at the beginning and a period at the end. They cannot "stand by themselves." (Occasionally, students may come across a writer who uses a dash to set off an extension that could "stand by itself" as a sentence. Sometimes, too, a writer will use dashes to set off an interruption that could "stand by itself." Those strategies are rare and will not be used in this book).

6. In 2004, FACEBOOK WAS A
    NEW SOCIAL MEDIA TOOL.   6. __B__

7. Ever since, FACEBOOK
    HAS GROWN EXPONENTIALLY. 7. __B__

8. ZUCKERBERG CREATED
    FACEBOOK, in 2004.   8. __D__

9. In the area of digital
    innovation, THE UNITED
    STATES HAS LED THE WAY. 9. _____

10. In the area of digital
    innovation, THE UNITED
    STATES HAS LED THE WAY—
    especially in the
    development of social
    media tools.   10. _____

11. THE UNITED STATES, in
    the area of digital
    innovation, HAS LED
    THE WAY.   11. _____

12. THE UNITED STATES IN
    THE AREA OF DIGITAL
    INNOVATION HAS LED
    THE WAY.   12. _____

13. In ranking the
    nation's top oil-
    producing states,
    TEXAS STILL TOPS
    NORTH DAKOTA.   13. _____

14. TEXAS STILL TOPS NORTH
    DAKOTA IN THE RANKING
    OF THE NATION'S TOP
    OIL-PRODUCING STATES.   14. _____

15. TEXAS, when it comes
    to domestic oil
    production, STILL TOPS
    NORTH DAKOTA.   15. _____

Exercise #2:

Subordination

SUBORDINATION

A. Main Part only

B. Introduction and Main Part

C. Interruption and Main Part

D. Extension and Main Part

E. Introduction, Interruption and Main Part

F. Introduction, Extension and Main Part

G. Interruption, Extension and Main Part

H. Intro., Interruption, Extension and Main Part

Directions: Choose the letter above that most accurately identifies the structure of the following sentences:

Note: Elements, of course, do not appear in sentences in the order indicated in each above. Only in B (intro., main part) and, sometimes, in E (intro., inter., MP) would that happen. In other words, the letters above identify the elements contained in the sentence—not the order in which they appear in the sentence.

Introductions: Most writers set off long introductions (anything longer than one prepositional phrase). But, for our purposes at least, whenever a long introduction is not set off, it should be considered a necessary modifier—not an introduction.

Many publisher stylebooks (guides for usage for specific publications) require a comma after the word "act," though some stylebooks would permit the writer to choose whether to use a comma or not.

At this point, it might be useful to identify some words that typically begin introductions. Here are a few:

after, although, as, as if, as long as, because, before, it, in, in order that, since, so that, though, unless, when, whenever, where, wherever, while, whoever, whomever, etc.

```
1.   When the president signed
     the Patriot Act, SEVERAL
     SENATORS VOICED STRONG
     RESERVATIONS.            1.   B

2.   WHEN THE PRESIDENT SIGNED
     THE PATRIOT ACT SEVERAL
     SENATORS VOICED STRONG
     RESERVATIONS.            2.   A
```

These words subordinate the elements which, when set off, should not be considered as part of the main part of the sentence.

Introductions with interruptions within them:

In the first sentence the comma after **Honolulu** begins the interruption—**Hawaii**—and the one after **Hawaii** ends it. The comma after **Hawaii** also ends the introduction; consequently the answer is E.

When there are several introductions, the second should be considered an interruption, if it is set off with commas:

Interruptions:

Aside from the interruptions within introductions that we have already observed, there are, of course, often interruptions within other elements of the sentence as well: within main parts, interruptions and extensions.

Again, if the writer chooses not to set off a segment, it should not be considered interruptive but a necessary modifier and a part of the main part of the sentence.

3. After a lengthy vacation in Honolulu, Hawaii, THE PRESIDENT RETURNED TO WASHINGTON.   3. __E__

4. After lengthy, and often stormy, debates in the Senate, THE BILL PASSED. 4. __E__

5. In 2011, when Arab president Hosni Mubarak was about to be ousted in a popular revolt, THE U.S. MAINTAINED A NEUTRAL POSITION ON WHETHER HE SHOULD REMAIN IN POWER.   5. __E__

6. When countries find it difficult to maintain their export levels or when other nations infringe on their markets, THE SITUATION IS CONSIDERED CRUCIAL TO NATIONAL INTEREST.   6. __B__

7. When countries find it difficult to maintain their export levels, when other nations infringe on their markets, THE SITUATION IS CONSIDERED CRUCIAL TO NATIONAL INTEREST.   7. __E__

8. When Obama proposed his plan, after careful consultation with his cabinet, THE CONGRESS WAS QUITE RECEPTIVE.   8. __E__

9. OBAMA, after meeting with his top aides, TOOK FULL RESPONSIBILITY.   9. __C__

10. OBAMA AFTER MEETING WITH HIS TOP AIDS TOOK FULL RESPONSIBILITY.   10. __A__

Interruptions, of course, can be used within interruptions. When, however, they create a situation in which too many commas are used too close together, dashes are generally used to set off the long interruption and commas are used to set off shorter interruptions within the longer interruptions. Sometimes, however, that structure is reversed: the shorter interruption is set off with dashes—usually for emphasis. Note the examples on the right:

Generally, interruptions end with the same mark they began with. If they begin with a comma, they should end with a comma. Sometimes, however, the dash will serve to end two interruptions—as in 12 and 14 here.

NOTE: Even though interruptions can occur within all sentence elements, that principal does not apply to other subordinate elements. Introductions cannot occur, for instance, within interruptions or extensions. If they do, they are considered interruptions of the sentence. Note the example to the right:

---

11. JOHN KERRY, meeting with Middle East leaders, in December 2013, to settle the Arab-Israeli dispute, RELIED ON HIS STAFF FOR UP-TO-DATE INFORMATION DURING THE TALKS. [Interruptions within interruptions—all set off with commas—do not seem confusing; commas are quite far apart and set off clear, distinct interruptions.]   11. ___C___

12. SOME FAMOUS ATHLETES—for instance, Tim McCarver, Orel Hershiser and Curt Schilling, all World Series champions—LATER BECAME WELL-KNOWN SPORTS BROADCASTERS. [Using all commas in such structures would often be confusing.] [A dash after "champions" serves to end both the interruption that began with a dash and the one that began with a comma.]   12. ___C___

13. OREL HERSHISER, who—in the 1988 season—pitched 59 straight scoreless innings, BECAME AN ANALYST FOR ESPN AND HAS CALLED SEVERAL LITTLE LEAGUE WORLD SERIES GAMES. [Dashes can appear within commas.] 13. ___C___

14. TIM MCCARVER, a catcher on the famous Cardinals teams of the 1960s—he caught the Hall-of-Famer Bob Gibson—BECAME AN ANALYST FOR FOX SPORTS AND HAS CALLED SEVERAL WORLD SERIES GAMES. [Dashes are often used to set off an abrupt interruption.]   14. ___C___

15. THE ST. LOUIS CARDINALS HAVE PRODUCED SOME FAMOUS PLAYERS OVER THE YEARS: for instance, Stan Musial is one of the greatest hitters of all time. ["For instance" should not be thought of as an introduction within the extension; it should be considered an interruption of the sentence; such an interpretation enables one to punctuate acceptably, and that is the object of this study and approach.] 15. ___G___

Using what you have learned from the examples above, identify the subordination in the following:

16. JIM BUNNING, who pitched two no-hitters in the major leagues, IS NOW A U.S. SENATOR FROM KENTUCKY.

16. _____

17. TWO PITCHERS WHO PLAYED TOGETHER FOR THE ATLANTA BRAVES, Tom Glavine and Greg Maddux, WERE ELECTED TO THE HALL OF FAME THE SAME YEAR.

17. _____

18. ATLANTA BRAVES PITCHERS TOM GLAVINE AND GREG MADDUX PLAYED TOGETHER AND WERE ELECTED TO THE HALL OF FAME THE SAME YEAR.

18. _____

19. A JAPANESE PLAYER, Ichiro Suzuki, WAS, of course, THE FIRST PLAYER TO COLLECT 4,000 HITS PLAYING IN THE TOP LEAGUES IN JAPAN AND THE UNITED STATES.

19. _____

20. A JAPANESE PLAYER, Ichiro Suzuki, WAS THE FIRST PLAYER TO COLLECT 4,000 HITS PLAYING IN THE TOP LEAGUES IN JAPAN AND THE UNITED STATES.

20. _____

21. HE HOLDS THE SEASON RECORD FOR HITS WITH 262, which he set in 2004.

21. _____

22. HE HOLDS THE SEASON RECORD FOR HITS WITH 262 WHICH HE SET IN 2004.

22. _____

23. THE FIRST JAPANESE PLAYER TO COLLECT 4,000 HITS, Ichiro Suzuki, an outfielder, REACHED THE MILESTONE WHILE PLAYING FOR THE NEW YORK YANKEES.

23. _____

24. THE FIRST JAPANESE PLAYER TO COLLECT 4,000 HITS, Ichiro Suzuki, REACHED THE MILESTONE WHILE PLAYING FOR THE NEW YORK YANKEES.

24. _____

25. On July 13 and 14, THE TWINS BEAT THE YANKEES IN TWO STRAIGHT GAMES.

25. _____

WRITING INSIGHTS: Discovering the Keys to Structure and Content

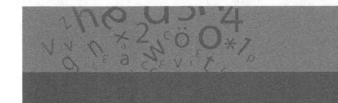

Exercise #3:

Subordination

sentences:

SUBORDINATION

A. Main Part only

B. Introduction and Main Part

C. Interruption and Main Part

D. Extension and Main Part

E. Introduction, Interruption and Main Part

F. Introduction, Extension and Main Part

G. Interruption, Extension and Main Part

H. Intro., Interruption, Extension and Main Part

Directions: Choose the letter above that most accurately identifies the structure of the following sentences:

Extensions: Very often writers "tack something on the end" of their sentences—a list, an explanation, an elaboration. Often, these extensions are set off with commas. But, when these extensions have commas within them, they are usually set off with dashes or colons. The colon is used for more formal extensions—such as lists or quotes. The dash is used for more abrupt extensions, usually for emphasis or for clarifying what is suggested or alluded to in the main sentence.

1. ONE CONTINENT HAS EXPERI-
    ENCED EXTREME POLITICAL
    CHANGE IN THE FIRST DECADE
    OF THIS CENTURY—Africa. [The
    dash clarifies by identifying
    the "one continent."]   1. __D__

2. THE GOVERNMENTS OF MANY NORTH
    AFRICAN NATIONS CHANGED
    DRASTICALLY, after the people
    forced out dictators who had
    ruled for decades.   2. __D__

3. After the people forced out
    dictators who had ruled for
    decades, THE GOVERNMENTS OF
    MANY NORTH AFRICAN NATIONS
    CHANGED DRASTICALLY.   3. __B__

4. THE GOVERNMENTS OF MANY NORTH
    AFRICAN NATIONS, after the
    people forced out dictators
    who had ruled for decades,   4. __C__
    CHANGED DRASTICALLY.

Note again that sometimes—but not always—subordinate elements can be any subordinate element: an introduction, interruption or extension—depending on where the writer places it in the sentence. For instance, "he said" expressions—added to direct or indirect quotes to identify the source—are usually set off with commas.

Partial quotes—that generally become part of the main sentence—are not usually set off with a comma.

Long introductory statements set off from the quote with a colon should be considered the main sentence. In those constructions, the quote—even though it is generally a sentence—should be looked upon as an extension.

Extensions often have interruptions within them—such as **for instance**, **of course**, **such as**, **for example**, and other interruptive phrases.

5. The UN Secretary General said, "THE ARAB SPRING HAS TRANSFORMED THE GEOPOLITICAL LANDSCAPE."

5. ___B___

6. "THE ARAB SPRING," he emphasized, "HAS TRANSFORMED THE GEOPOLITICAL LANDSCAPE."

6. ___C___

7. "THE ARAB SPRING HAS TRANSFORMED THE GEOPOLITICAL LANDSCAPE," said Ban Ki-moon in his year-end briefing.

7. ___D___

8. "THE ARAB SPRING HAS TRANSFORMED THE GEOPOLITICAL LANDSCAPE," said Ban Ki-moon, the UN Secretary General.

8. ___D___

9. BAN KI-MOON SAID THAT THE WORLD IS "AT AN INFLECTION POINT IN HISTORY."

9. ___A___

10. BAN KI-MOON COMMENTED ABOUT THE SIGNIFICANCE OF THE ARAB SPRING: "This is the moment which we have to seize and help them."

10. ___D___

11. AFRICA HAS SOME EXTREMELY IMPORTANT NATURAL RESOURCES: diamonds, for instance, and most of the world's cobalt.

11. ___G___

12. AFRICA HAS MUCH OF THE WORLD'S MOST VALUABLE METAL: such as, copper, gold, manganese and uranium.

12. ___G___

Writers at times choose not to set off expressions like **such as**; when they do set them off, however, the expressions should be considered an interruption. The commas after **copper** and **gold** are used to separate parts of a series, as will be noted in the next unit on coordination.

Just as the second of two introductions separated by a comma should be considered an interruption (see 5 and 7 in Exercise 2), so should the first of two expressions be considered an interruption in a sense. They both interrupt the sentence and such an interpretation helps one to punctuate such structures acceptably.

Using what you have learned so far, provide answers for sentences 15 through 20.

NOTE: Most stylebooks require only one space after colons—not two.

13. AFRICA HAS MUCH OF THE WORLD'S MOST VALUABLE MET- AL: such as copper, gold, manganese and uranium.

13. ___D___

14. SOUTH AFRICA HOLDS A SIG- NIFICANT PORTION OF THE WORLD'S MOST PRECIOUS METAL—gold, to be exact.

14. ___D___

15. In 2011, THE PEOPLE OUST- ED DICTATORS IN SEVERAL NORTH AFRICAN NATIONS: Egypt, Tunisia, Libya and Yemen.

15. _____

16. MANY AFRICAN NATIONS, however, HAVE STRUGGLED TO BECOME FREE SINCE BE- ING GRANTED INDEPENDENCE FROM THE MAJOR EUROPEAN COLONIAL POWERS: England and France.

16. _____

17. After they ousted their dictators, MOST OF THE NATIONS ATTEMPTED TO ES- TABLISH DEMOCRATIC GOVERN- MENTS.

17. _____

18. MANY OF THESE NEW DEMOC- RACIES, however, HAVE GOTTEN OFF TO SHAKY STARTS.

18. _____

19. EGYPT, for instance, RE- VERTED TO MILITARY RULE IN 2013.

19. _____

20. LIBYA, for instance, ELECTED A GENERAL NATION- AL CONGRESS IN 2012 BUT HAS YET TO DRAFT A PERMA- NENT CONSTITUTION.

20. _____

Exercise #4:

Subordination

SUBORDINATION

A. Main Part only

B. Introduction and Main Part

C. Interruption and Main Part

D. Extension and Main Part

E. Introduction, Interruption and Main Part

F. Introduction, Extension and Main Part

G. Interruption, Extension and Main Part

H. Intro., Interruption, Extension and Main Part

Directions: In the blanks provided, place the letter from above which identifies the pattern of the sentence following the number.

Note: To illustrate that sentences have main parts and subordinate parts, the main parts of the sentences in this exercise will be in all caps.

---

(1) In the history of the NFL, ONLY FOUR TEAMS HAVE WON THE SUPER BOWL AT LEAST FOUR TIMES: the Pittsburgh Steelers, the San Francisco Forty-niners, the Green Bay Packers and the Dallas Cowboys. (2) THE STEELERS WERE THE FIRST TO DO SO. (3) In 1975, THEY BEAT THE VIKINGS FOR THEIR FIRST TITLE. THEY WON THEIR FOURTH IN 1979. (4) Since then, THEY HAVE WON TWO MORE SUPER BOWLS FOR A TOTAL OF SIX TITLES. (5) THE FORTY-NINERS AND THE COWBOYS HAVE EACH WON FIVE SUPER BOWLS WHILE THE PACK-ERS HAVE WON FOUR. (6) THE PACKERS, it could be ar-gued, HAVE HAD THE MOST CONSISTENT SUCCESS IN THE SUPER BOWL ERA—winning the first Super Bowl ever played, in 1966, and their most recent title in 2010.

(7) However, WINNING THE SUPER BOWL—the champion-ship game between the AFC and the NFC champions—ISN'T

1. _____

2. _____

3. _____

4. _____

5. _____

6. _____

7. _____

EASY. (8) ONE MAJOR FACTOR HAS PREVENTED ANY SINGLE FRANCHISE FROM DOMINATING THE BIG GAME—parity. (9) SOME PLAYERS, known as "restricted" free agents, CAN SIGN WITH OTHER TEAMS AFTER BEING IN THE LEAGUE FOR JUST THREE YEARS. (10) Often, THAT LEADS TO PLAYERS LEAVING THE TEAMS THAT DRAFTED THEM FOR LUCRATIVE OFFERS ELSE-WHERE, meaning that many players will play for several teams during their careers. (11) DRAFT SLOTS ALSO ENSURE THAT POOR TEAMS HAVE A CHANCE TO PICK FROM THE TOP PROS-PECTS FROM COLLEGE, virtually ensuring that teams will go through cycles of winning and losing.

(12) IT WAS DIFFERENT IN THE EARLY DAYS OF THE NFL. (13) THE MINNESOTA VIKINGS, for instance, MADE IT TO FOUR SUPER BOWLS—losing all four, by the way—WITH MANY OF THE SAME PLAYERS ON EACH TEAM, such as Jim Marshall, Alan Page and Mick Tingelhoff. (14) THE FORTY-NINERS, mean-while, WON FOUR SUPER BOWLS IN THE 1980S WITH THE SAME QUARTERBACK AT THE HELM: Joe Montana.

(15) Indeed, if there is one position that seems to be of utmost importance in winning Super Bowls, IT IS THE QUARTERBACK. (16) SEVERAL QUARTERBACKS HAVE, over the years, WON MORE THAN ONE SUPER BOWL GAME. (17) THEY INCLUDE MONTANA, BART STARR, TERRY BRADSHAW, TROY AIKMAN AND TOM BRADY. (18) STILL OTHERS HAVE APPEARED IN MORE THAN ONE SUPER BOWL WITHOUT WINNING ONE OF THEM, includ-ing Fran Tarkenton, Jim Kelly and Craig Morton. (19) THE QUARTERBACK POSITION SEEMS TO BE MORE IMPORTANT THAN EVER. At the same time, THE POSITION SEEMS TO GET MORE COMPLICATED WITH EACH PASSING SEASON. (20) For instance, TARKENTON—who led the Vikings to three Super Bowl games in the 1970s—OFTEN CALLED THE PLAYS HIMSELF, rather than relying on a coach. (21) Today, OFFENSIVE COORDINATORS CHOOSE PLAYS FROM A VAST LIST OF CHOICES AND RELAY THOSE PLAYS TO THE QUARTERBACK. (22) MANY PLAYS—some with five receivers—ARE ALSO VERY COMPLEX.

(23) So, IT'S NOT EASY TO WIN A SUPER BOWL. (24) ONLY A FEW TEAMS HAVE HAD SUSTAINED SUCCESS—often those with excellent quarterbacks who could master difficult schemes and plays. (25) With parity the name of the game, THAT LIKELY WON'T CHANGE ANYTIME SOON.

8. _____
9. _____
10. _____
11. _____
12. _____
13. _____
14. _____
15. _____
16. _____
17. _____
18. _____
19. _____
20. _____
21. _____
22. _____
23. _____
24. _____
25. _____

Note: Commas within the extension in sentences 1, 13 and 18 and within the main part in sentence 17 are used to set off parts of a series (see Chapter 2: Insight #2).

Exercise #5:

Subordination

SUBORDINATION

A. Main Part only

B. Introduction and Main Part

C. Interruption and Main Part

D. Extension and Main Part

E. Introduction, Interruption and Main Part

F. Introduction, Extension and Main Part

G. Interruption, Extension and Main Part

H. Intro., Interruption, Extension and Main Part

Directions: In the blanks provided, place the letter from above which identifies the pattern of the sentence following the number:

Note: Now the main part is not in all caps, so remember that the main part of the sentence is that part of the sentence which can "stand by itself." The subordinate elements—the introduction, interruption and extension—are separated from the main part with commas, dashes or colons.

---

(1) The year 2011 was one of the most important, historically, for the modern Arab world. (2) In that year alone, four countries—Egypt, Libya, Tunisia and Yemen—overthrew dictators who had held power for decades. (3) In some sense, it was a major democratic revolution, though whether those countries will emerge with functioning free governments remains to be determined. (4) But the signs are promising.

(5) Tunisian president Zine El Abidine Ben Ali was the first to fall, overthrown on January 14, 2011. (6) About one month later, on February 11, Egyptian President Hosni Mubarak resigned. (7) Then, in August, rebel forces overtook Tripoli, putting an end to the reign of Muammar Gaddafi. (8) Finally, on February 27, 2012, Yemeni president Ali Abdullah Saleh gave up power.

1. _____
2. _____
3. _____
4. _____
5. _____
6. _____
7. _____
8. _____

(9) Much of this was accomplished by what scholars call "people power"—nonviolent protests and other acts of civil disobedience. (10) For instance, thousands of protestors gathered in Cairo's Tahrir Square every day for months, demanding that Mubarak step down. (11) In Tunisia, the first protests broke out in the city of Sidi Bouzid after a man named Mohamed Bouazizi set himself on fire to protest police corruption and mistreatment. (12) In Libya, NATO intervention—after the government had violently cracked down on protestors—led to Gaddafi's overthrow. (13) He was killed by a mob after being captured in his hometown of Sirte. (14) Indeed, one characteristic each of these countries shared was mass protest. (15) Some of the largest protests in these countries with large Muslim populations, in fact, occurred regularly during Friday prayer sessions.

(16) Social media has been credited for helping the protests gain momentum. (17) In the early days of the Egyptian uprising, for instance, organizers published their plans on Facebook pages, generating huge turnouts to Tahrir Square. (18) They also used Twitter to send messages during rallies, letting followers know where, specifically, to gather and how to avoid police or security forces. (19) In fact, a study by The University of Washington found that social media played a central role in shaping political debates in the Arab Spring and that conversations about revolution often preceded major events. (20) The study showed that during the week before Mubarak's resignation, the rate of tweets from Egypt—and around the world—about political change in that country ballooned from 2,300 a day to 230,000 a day. (21) Little of this organization would have been possible even five years earlier when social media was still in its infancy. (22) The technology proved to be invaluable for the needs of the time.

(23) Some writers have even referred to the emergence of a "digital democracy" that allows activists to get around the limitations and restrictions of autocratic governments. (24) Besides Facebook and Twitter, for instance, people used cell phones to take pictures and communicate during demonstrations. (25) For many people in these repressed countries, it was the first chance they had to participate in a meaningful discussion about the future of their society.

9. _____
10. _____
11. _____
12. _____
13. _____
14. _____
15. _____
16. _____
17. _____
18. _____
19. _____
20. _____
21. _____
22. _____
23. _____
24. _____
25. _____

Note: Commas within the interruption in sentence 2 are used to set off parts of a series (see Chapter 2: Insight #2).

Exercise #6:

Subordination

Directions: Write sentences that have the following subordinate elements in addition to the main part. Underline the subordinate parts as is done in the examples. Students will find it helpful to write sentences first on scratch paper. Also, it is helpful to begin with the main part of the sentences. Then add the requested subordination.

Example: Using movies as subject matter, write a sentence that has <u>an introduction</u> and <u>an interruption</u>—in addition to the main part:

> <u>In recent years,</u> movies aimed at teenagers, <u>such as vampire films,</u> have been very popular.

Example: Using the military as subject matter, write a sentence that has <u>an introduction</u> and <u>an extension</u>—in addition to the main part:

> <u>When young people consider careers,</u> they should not overlook the U.S. Army, <u>which offers a great variety of job opportunities.</u>

Example: Using sports as subject matter, write a sentence that has <u>an introduction</u> and <u>an interruption</u>—in addition to the main part:

Example: Using education as subject matter, write a sentence that has <u>an interruption</u> and <u>an extension</u>—in addition to the main part

Example: Using TV as subject matter, write a sentence that has <u>an introduction</u>, <u>an interruption</u> and <u>an extension</u>—in addition to the main part.

Example: Using money as subject matter, write a sentence that has <u>an interruption</u>—in addition to the main part.

Example: Using politics as subject matter, write a sentence that has <u>an introduction</u>—in addition to the main part.

Note: Information in these exercises need not be accurate, but it should be plausible.

NOTES

Exercise #7:

Subordination

Directions: To develop awareness of introductions, interruptions and extensions, find examples of the following in newspapers or magazines or their Web sites. Cut out or print copies of the examples and place them in the spaces provided. Place parentheses around the sentence that contains the requested subordinate elements and underline these elements as is done in the examples. (Sentences may contain more subordinate elements than requested but underline only those asked for).

Introduction and Main Part (example)

(<u>In the aftermath of the worst flooding in the county's history</u>, officials are considering proposals to build levees that will protect large tracts of farmland.)

Intro., Ext., and Main Part (example)

(<u>Over the past three decades</u>, the journalist Thomas Friedman has reported from some of the world's most complicated places—<u>beginning with the Middle East</u>.)

Main Part only

Introduction, Interruption and Main Part

Introduction and Main Part

Introduction, Extension and Main Part

Interruption and Main Part

Interruption, Extension and Main Part

Extension and Main Part

Intro., Inter., Ext. and Main Part

Insight #2:

Parallelism

Another major aspect of sentence structure that professional writers understand, in addition to subordination, is coordination (or what is sometimes called parallelism). This consists of the doubling of words, phrases, clauses or other word groups in what is called a <u>compound</u> and the tripling or more of these elements in what is called a <u>series</u>.

Consequently, an important insight that students of writing must acquire—insofar as sentence structure is concerned—is an awareness of coordination: the acceptable repetition of elements within the sentence.

INSIGHT #2: ***Sentence Structure***: Writers often consciously double or triple elements within sentences, know how to punctuate them acceptably and keep them alike grammatically.

In addition to recognizing subordination, the student of writing must also develop a consciousness of coordination in sentences—more commonly called parallelism.

Elements in English sentences—main parts, subordinate parts or parts of each—may be doubled (a compound), tripled, quadrupled, etc. (a series). Students of writing must become aware of this repeating of elements because of coordination—the need to keep elements alike grammatically (parallel)—and because of certain conventions (practices) of punctuation that writers are required to observe when using a compound or a series.

Exercise #8:

Coordination

To develop an awareness of coordination in writing, the student should note that every sentence has one of the following four structures, insofar as parallelism is concerned:

A. No parallelism   C. Series (more than two)

B. Compound (two)   D. Compound and Series

Directions: Match the sentences on the right with the most appropriate letter above:

Note: In the following examples, parallel elements will be underlined. Some examples will be answered and explained to emphasize some of the practices writers tend to follow in handling parallelism.

Note: The commas after United States in sentence 2 and oil in sentence 3 are used to separate parts of a series—not to set off an introduction, interruption or extension.

    Repetition of one-word elements—such as the nouns and adjectives to the right—is familiar to most students and does not pose a problem. Longer elements, however, are more difficult to recognize and keep parallel.

    The elements are parallel because the writer began each with parallel expressions: "the first to launch" and "the first to place."

1. The <u>United States</u> and <u>Russia</u> were the first countries to explore space. 1. __B__

2. The <u>United States</u>, <u>Russia</u> and <u>China</u> were the first countries to develop nuclear bombs. 2. __C__

3. <u>Russia</u> and the <u>U.S.</u> are trying to find new <u>oil</u>, <u>iron</u> and <u>copper</u> deposits in arctic regions. 3. __D__

4. The Russians were <u>the first to launch an artificial satellite</u> and <u>the first to place a manned spaceship in orbit</u>. 4. __B__

5. <u>On October 4, 1957, they launched the first artificial satellite, Sputnik I</u>; <u>on April 12, 1961, they placed the first man in space, Yuri Gagarin</u>. 5. __B__

Sometimes the whole sentence is repeated (a compound sentence). In such sentences, either a semicolon (;) or a comma and a coordinate conjunction (, and; , but; , or; , for; etc.) may be used to separate the two sentences. Notice all the parts of sentence 5 that are alike (parallel): the dates, the verbs and the extensions. Writers deliberately keep parallel elements and sentences grammatically alike as much as possible.

All three elements underlined in sentence 6 can grammatically follow the verb improve; they are parallel.

The comma before and that separates the last two parts of a series is usually omitted. Sometimes even the and is omitted, if the sentence seems to read well enough without it. Notice its omission in the next example:

Since repeated elements should be coordinated (kept grammatically alike as possible), writers find it helpful to start parallel elements with the same or similar words. Note that in sentence 7 the parallel elements all start with the same words—"the first."

When the main part of a sentence is noted (as with all capital letters in sentences 8 and 9), one can see that parallelism can be used in any sentence element.

Notice, too, how parallelism can become rather complicated. In sentence 10, a series is a part of a compound element.

Remember: Many sentences, even long ones, often do not have parallel elements.

6. Space exploration has enabled man to improve weather forecasting, communication systems and mapping practices. 6. __C__

7. Russia has accumulated a number of firsts in space: the first artificial satellite, the first man in space, the first woman in space, the first on-land space recovery system. 7. __C__

8. On December 24 and 25, ASTRONAUTS FRANK BORMAN, WILLIAM ANDERS AND JAMES LOVELL ORBITED THE MOON TEN TIMES. 8. __D__

9. On December 24 and 25, THREE U.S. ASTRONAUTS—Frank Borman, William Anders and James Lovell—ORBITED THE MOON TEN TIMES. 9. __D__

10. Scientists hope that space travel will answer two persistent questions about the universe: how were the sun, the planets and the stars formed and whether life exists in space. 10. __D__

11. No doubt man's most spectacular space feat occurred when Neil Armstrong first set foot on the moon, July 20, 1969. 11. __A__

From what you have learned so far, answer the following:

Note: As you have no doubt noted, in sentences in this booklet, the comma is not used before the <u>and</u>, <u>or</u>, <u>nor</u>, <u>but</u>, etc., that are often used to separate the last two parts of a series. **Most publications do not use the comma in that way.** It is generally used with <u>and</u> and other coordinate conjunctions only when it separates two complete sentences—when it is used instead of a period and a capital letter or a semicolon—or when it is used in a series whose elements contain commas.

12. Man explores space primarily <u>to make new discoveries in the universe</u> and <u>to utilize space to serve needs here on earth</u>.   12. _____

13. New discoveries in space have included <u>detection of the Van Allen radiation belt</u>, <u>the density of meteors in space</u> and <u>the depth of ozone in the earth's atmosphere</u>.   13. _____

14. Three U.S. astronauts—<u>Neil Armstrong</u>, <u>Edwin Aldrin</u> and <u>Michael Collins</u>—were aboard the famous Apollo 11 lunar flight that put <u>Armstrong</u> and <u>Aldrin</u> on the moon.   14. _____

15. The Apollo 11 flight <u>to the moon</u> and <u>back again</u> took <u>195 hours</u> and <u>18 minutes</u>.   15. _____

16. The second lunar landing mission, the Apollo 12 flight, placed a lunar module on the moon, November 19, 1969, not more than 600 feet from the first one placed there by the Apollo 11 mission.   16. _____

17. <u>Charles Conrad</u> and <u>Alan Bean</u> reached the moon on Apollo 12's lunar module, the Intrepid.   17. _____

18. In addition to the first lunar landing made July 20, 1969, by <u>Armstrong</u> and <u>Aldrin</u>, three more were made before the end of 1971: on <u>November 19, 1969</u>, <u>February 5, 1971</u>, and <u>July 30, 1971</u>.   18. _____

19. Lunar modules, more commonly known as LMs, carry two people to the surface of the moon.   19. _____

20. <u>The most famous lunar module, of course, was the Eagle, the first to place men on the moon</u>; but <u>there were others that brought men to the moon, too: the Intrepid, the Antares and the Falcon</u>.   20. _____

Name _____ **Date** _____

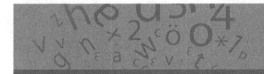

Exercise #9:

Subordination-Coordination

SUBORDINATION

A. Main Part only

B. Introduction and Main Part

C. Interruption and Main Part

D. Extension and Main Part

E. Intro., Inter., MP

F. Intro., Ext., MP

G. Inter., Ext., MP

H. Intro., Inter., Ext., MP

PARALLELISM

A. No parallelism

B. Compound

C. Series

D. Compound & Series

Directions: In the blanks provided, place the letter from above which identifies the pattern of the sentence following the number.

Note: In these exercises, it may be easier to do one column at a time. Do the subordination first; then go back and do the coordination—the parallelism.

---

(1) ONE OF THE MOST REVOLUTIONARY DIGITAL ME-DIA COMPANIES CREATED IN THE LATE 20th CENTURY WAS GOOGLE. (2) GOOGLE BEGAN AS A SEARCH ENGINE—an Internet device that allows people to <u>enter key words</u> and <u>receive links</u> to Web information. (3) THAT, alone, REVOLUTIONIZED HOW PEOPLE USED THE INTERNET. (4) BUT THE COMPANY HAS BECOME SO MUCH MORE.

(5) GOOGLE WAS FOUNDED BY <u>LARRY PAGE</u> AND <u>SERGEY BRIN</u> WHILE THEY WERE Ph.D. STUDENTS AT STANFORD UNIVERSITY—the school in California's Silicon Valley that has become associated with the high-tech digital age.

(6) ITS RISE FROM DIGITAL START-UP TO MULTI-NATIONAL CORPORATION WAS FAST. (7) On September

	Sub	Para
1.	_____	_____
2.	_____	_____
3.	_____	_____
4.	_____	_____
5.	_____	_____
6.	_____	_____
7.	_____	_____

4, 1998, GOOGLE WAS INCORPORATED AS A PRIVATE-
LY HELD COMPANY. (8) THAT WAS FOLLOWED SEVERAL
YEARS LATER—on August 19, 2004—WITH AN INITIAL
PUBLIC OFFERING. (9) By 2011, THE NUMBER OF
UNIQUE MONTHLY VISITORS TO GOOGLE HAD TOPPED ONE
BILLION. (10) THE COMPANY EARNED $50 BILLION IN
2012.

(11) GOOGLE BEGAN IN 1996 AS A RESEARCH
PROJECT. (12) However, PAGE AND BRIN, who ini-
tially called their creation BackRub, WERE CLEAR
ABOUT WHAT THEY THOUGHT THEY COULD ACCOMPLISH.
(13) THE COMPANY'S MISSION STATEMENT WAS TO "OR-
GANIZE THE WORLD'S INFORMATION AND MAKE IT UNI-
VERSALLY ACCESSIBLE AND USEFUL." (14) Its unoffi-
cial slogan: "DON'T BE EVIL."

(15) Since it went public, GOOGLE HAS
BOUGHT SEVERAL OTHER COMPANIES IN AN EFFORT TO
EXPAND ITS DIGITAL OFFERINGS AND REACH. (16) To-
day, ITS APPLICATIONS INCLUDE EMAIL, AN OFFICE
SUITE AND A SOCIAL NETWORKING SITE. (17) DESKTOP
PRODUCTS INCLUDE APPLICATIONS FOR WEB BROWSING,
PHOTO ORGANIZING AND INSTANT MESSAGING.

(18) PERHAPS ITS MOST GROUNDBREAKING PROD-
UCT, however, IS GOOGLE GLASS—a computer with a
display that is worn on the head. (19) THE COM-
PUTER ATTACHES TO EYEGLASS FRAMES, DISPLAYS IN-
FORMATION HANDS-FREE AND RESPONDS TO VOICE COM-
MANDS. (20) In November 2012, *TIME* MAGAZINE
CHOSE GOOGLE GLASS AS ONE OF THE BEST INVENTIONS
OF THE YEAR. (21) THE U.S. AIR FORCE WAS TESTING
GOOGLE GLASS FOR POSSIBLE MILITARY USE. (22) RE-
SEARCHERS SAID THE DEVICE COULD ALSO BE USED FOR
SEARCH AND RESCUE MISSIONS AND TO HELP AIR TRAF-
FIC CONTROLLERS, among other things.

(23) Yes, GOOGLE HAS COME A LONG WAY FROM
ITS BEGINNINGS AS A SEARCH ENGINE. (24) NO DOUBT
THE COMPANY WILL CREATE MORE DEVICES THAT REVOLU-
TIONIZE THE WAY PEOPLE LIVE AND COMMUNICATE.

8. _____ _____

9. _____ _____
10. _____ _____

11. _____ _____
12. _____ _____

13. _____ _____

14. _____ _____

15. _____ _____

16. _____ _____

17. _____ _____

18. _____ _____

19. _____ _____

20. _____ _____

21. _____ _____
22. _____ _____

23. _____ _____
24. _____ _____

It's important to know how to punctuate <u>however</u>. Is it *however* or *,however* or *; however,*? It depends on the structure—the design—of the sentence.

If <u>however</u> merely interrupts a sentence—as it does in sentence 18 in Exercise 9—it is set off with commas. In that sentence, <u>however</u> interrupts the main part of a sentence that includes an interruption (the "however") and an extension.

When <u>however</u> begins the second part of a compound sentence, a semicolon precedes it:

Example: Egypt established a democracy soon after the Arab Spring overthrew longstanding President Hosni Mubarak; however, the military later ousted an elected president and again assumed power.

In such a sentence, <u>however</u> should not be considered an introduction. It should be considered an interruption. It does not introduce the long compound sentence—which it would have to do to be considered an introduction for the sentence. It does in a sense, however, interrupt the whole sentence—the compound sentence. So, the answer should be C, if such a sentence appears in one of the exercises in this book.

When <u>however</u> is used as a verb—a necessary modifier—it is not set off:

Example: However long the game lasts, he will stay until it ends

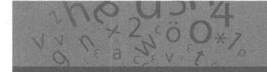

Exercise #10:

Subordination-Coordination

SUBORDINATION		**PARALLELISM**
A. Main Part only	E. Intro., Inter., MP	A. No parallelism
B. Introduction and Main Part	F. Intro., Ext., MP	B. Compound
C. Interruption and Main Part	G. Inter., Ext., MP	C. Series
D. Extension and Main Part	H. Intro., Inter., Ext., MP	D. Compound & Series

Directions: In the blanks provided, place the letter from above which identifies the pattern of the sentence following the number.

Note: In these exercises, it may be easier to do one column at a time. Do the subordination first; then go back and do the coordination—the parallelism.

---

(1) One of the most promising revolutions of the early 21st Century was the Arab Spring—a series of popular revolts in North Africa and the Middle East that led to the demise of four autocratic regimes. (2) A long list of social ills led to these uprisings: political repression, government corruption, high unemployment, a general lack of personal freedom. (3) But most observers considered them to be, broadly speaking, democracy movements.

(4) In the early days of the Arab Spring, it was popular to assume that the countries that had thrown off undemocratic and harsh rule would soon become free and democratic. (5) Indeed, Egypt, Tunisia, Yemen and Libya all wrote constitutions and held elections after their liberation.

(6) Unfortunately, the strength of these emerging democracies has waned, leaving them without the strong democratic government that the United States and the Western world had hoped for.

	Sub	Para
1.	_____	_____
2.	_____	_____
3.	_____	_____
4.	_____	_____
5.	_____	_____
6.	_____	_____

---

(7) In the wake of the protests, Egypt threw out President Hosni Mubarak—who had held power for 30 years—drafted a constitution and elected a new president: Mohamed Morsi. (8) However, in 2013, the Egyptian army threw out Morsi—a leader of an Islamist group called the Muslim Brotherhood—in favor of military rule. (9) While many in the West cheered this development because of the unpopularity of the Muslim Brotherhood, it does suggest how difficult it will be for Egyptians to hold and enforce elections.

(10) Libyans, meanwhile, elected a General National Assembly after the ouster of the dictator Muammar Gaddafi. (11) That assembly was then handed power by an interim government on August 8, 2012. (12) But that arrangement, too, has been marred by instability. (13) About a month after that transfer of power, Islamic militants attacked the American consulate in Benghazi, killing American ambassador J. Christopher Stevens in an event that soon came to symbolize Libyan dysfunction and hostility to the West since Gaddafi's ouster. (14) Regional warlords and clans remain a problem to the government.

(15) Yemen has seen much violence since its transition from authoritarianism to democracy. (16) On November 23, 2011, president Ali Abdullah Saleh flew to Saudi Arabia and signed a plan to provide for the transfer of political power in Yemen. (17) He initially relinquished power to his deputy, Vice President Abd Rabbuh Mansur Hadi. (18) Hadi won a presidential election in February 2012, formed a unity government and prepared to oversee the drafting of a new constitution. (19) Yet despite those developments toward a freer Yemen, terrorist attacks in the country—including on the presidential palace—have hindered the country's progress.

(20) Tunisia, perhaps, offers the most hopeful chance for real democratic reform among the countries involved in the Arab Spring. (21) That is fitting, since the Arab Spring is thought to have begun in Tunisia when a 26-year-old street vendor named Mohamed Bouazizi set himself on fire to protest his treatment by a city official. (22) That act led to the popular revolt that ultimately toppled longtime President Zine El Abidine Ben Ali, who had held power for 23 years. (23) In March 2011, the country held elections to a constituent assembly—elections that international observers deemed free and fair. (24) A political party known as the Ennahda Movement, which had been banned under Ben Ali's regime, won 90 of 217 seats.

7. _____ _____

8. _____ _____

9. _____ _____

10. _____ _____

11. _____ _____

12. _____ _____
13. _____ _____

14. _____ _____

15. _____ _____

16. _____ _____

17. _____ _____

18. _____ _____

19. _____ _____

20. _____ _____

21. _____ _____

22. _____ _____

23. _____ _____

24. _____ _____

PUNCTUATION

As noted in Chapter 1, most punctuation is used to set off subordinate elements (added modifiers) from the main part of the sentence. Also, some punctuation is used to separate parts of coordinate elements—especially three or more equal (parallel) elements in a row (a series).

The first two chapters—on subordination and coordination—hopefully have helped students develop some awareness of structure and the part punctuation plays in writing sentences. The reader, as a mere consumer of writing, need not be aware of punctuation and, indeed, is oftan not aware of it. The writer, however, as a producer of sentences to be read, must be conscious of the structure of sentences and the part punctuation plays in producing them.

SUBORDINATION: COMMAS, DASHES, COLONS

There are three punctuation marks generally used to set off subordinate elements: the comma (,), the dash (—), and the colon (:).

The **comma** is used the most extensively—since it is often used to set off all three subordinate elements: introductions, interruptions and extensions.

The **dash** (—) is used extensively, too—since it is often used to set off both interruptions and extensions that are usually abrupt, contain commas or need to be emphasized. Only occasionally, however, is the dash used to set off an introduction—and then only if it is extremely long and complicated with a great deal of internal punctuation—or if the introduction is a long series of introductory statements.

The **colon** (:) is used the least. It sets off only one subordinate element—the extension. It is never used to set off an introduction or an interruption from the main part of the sentence. To make the colon even less needed, the dash can be, and often is, used to set off extensions. The colon seems to be preferred, however, in formal writing—especially to set off lists and quotes that are used as extensions.

COORDINATION: COMMAS, SEMICOLONS

Again, the <u>comma</u> (,) is most frequently used between parts of a series. It separates the equal (coordinated) parts not separated by <u>and</u> or some other coordinate conjunction—<u>but</u>, <u>or</u>, <u>for</u>, <u>nor</u>, etc.

Occasionally, the semicolon (;) needs to be used to separate parts of a series—especially when a part, several parts or all parts of a series are complicated or contain commas.

Examples:
- The officers selected were Harry Nellis, president; George Harris, secretary; and John Mills, treasurer.
- Three noted Scandinavian scientists explored the remote arctic island: Sigvald Torson, a Swedish oceanographer; Thorvald Hanscom, a Norwegian archaeologist, and Bernt Bjornson, a Danish physicist.

[In the second example, either a comma or a semicolon can be used before <u>and</u>; no strong convention or practice has emerged. Every writer chooses one and sticks to it.]

Also, the semicolon (;) is often used to separate two sentences or the two parts of a compound sentence when they are not separated by <u>and</u> or some other coordinate conjunction. Often in these cases, the content of the two "sentences" on either side of the semicolon are closely related. In such instances, it is helpful to think of the semicolon as the equivalent of a period and a capital letter that starts a new sentence. (In rare cases, writers will use a colon (:) to set off an extension that is essentially a main part—usually when the material after the colon is alluded to before the colon and can be anticipated).

Examples:
- Exploration of space is important; it is needed for technological development.
- Exploration of space is important; therefore, the government feels justified in fully supporting space projects.
- Space projects are essential to technological development; and, if the United States is to keep pace with other leading world powers, it must promote an extensive space program.

[In the second example a comma after <u>therefore</u> is optional.]

[In the third example, a semicolon often precedes <u>and</u> when it separates two sentences with punctuation in each].

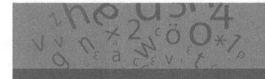

Exercise #11:

Punctuation

PUNCTUATION MARK USED:

A. Comma

B. Semicolon

C. Colon

D. Dash

E. Generally no punctuation needed

WHY PUNCTUATION MARK IS NEEDED:

A. To set off introduction

B. To set off interruption

C. To set off extension

D. To separate parts of a series

E. To separate independent clauses [sentences]

F. None [for E above]

Directions: Use the most appropriate letter above for the numbers below:

```
        One of the most famous photographs to emerge        Punct.   Why?
from the Obama Administration pictured the Pres-
ident (1) and his advisors during the raid that      1. _____  _____
killed Osama bin Laden.  In the photo (2) the Pres-  2. _____  _____
ident sits in the corner (3) elbows on knees—watch-  3. _____  _____
ing the raid on a television screen.   Vice Presi-
dent Joe Biden sits in front of him, arms crossed
(4) while Secretary of State Hillary Clinton sits    4. _____  _____
on the other side of the room with one hand cov-
ering her mouth.  The photo was taken before bin
Laden was captured (5) one of the most important     5. _____  _____
moments in the war on terror.
        A philosopher once said (6) that a picture   6. _____  _____
is worth a thousand words (7) that seems like an     7. _____  _____
appropriate sentiment for this photograph.  The
intensity of the moment (8) clearly shows on the     8. _____  _____
faces of the President and his inner circle (9) in-  9. _____  _____
cluding Clinton, Defense Secretary Robert Gates and
```

```
Chief of Staff Denis McDonough.  Moreover (10)      10. _____  _____
the faces all peer intently in the same direction
(11) symbolizing the sheer focus on the mission      11. _____  _____
at hand.
     A group of Navy SEALS—highly trained
stealth fighters (12) pulled off the raid.  In       12. _____  _____
some ways (13) it was an unlikely feat (14)          13. _____  _____
Obama (15) himself (16) confessed later that he      14. _____  _____
had doubts about whether the raid would work.        15. _____  _____
It did.  At the moment this famous photograph        16. _____  _____
was taken (17) however (18) it was unclear what      17. _____  _____
would happen.  The political implications (19)       18. _____  _____
could have been catastrophic for the president.      19. _____  _____
Had the raid not succeeded, it could have hurt
Obama's chances in the 2012 election (20) just as    20. _____  _____
the failed rescue of U.S. hostages in Iran had
hurt President Jimmy Carter's campaign in 1980.
Moreover (21) a botched raid could have embold-      21. _____  _____
ened al-Qaida (22) the terror group led by bin       22. _____  _____
Laden (23) and other radical organizations.          23. _____  _____
     No one knew (24) what the outcome would be      24. _____  _____
and this famous photograph captures that moment
in time.
```

Note: For some sentences, more than one answer is possible. Number 5, for instance, could be a comma or a dash, though a dash is the most effective option. Number 13 could be a comma or no punctuation, though a comma would provide greater clarity. Number 20, meanwhile, could be a comma or a dash, though a dash would serve to set off the extension with greater emphasis. Finally, commas would work for 22 and 23, though dashes would serve to emphasize the phrase "the terror group led by bin Laden."

Exercise #12:

Punctuation

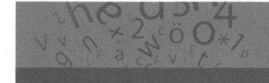

PUNCTUATION MARK USED:	WHY PUNCTUATION MARK IS NEEDED:
A. Comma	A. To set off introduction
B. Semicolon	B. To set off interruption
C. Colon	C. To set off extension
D. Dash	D. To separate parts of a series
E. Generally no punctuation needed	E. To separate independent clauses [sentences]
	F. None [for E above]

Directions: Use the most appropriate letter above for the numbers below:

```
        Of the many social media innovations of the      Punct.   Why?
early 21st Century (1) Facebook is probably the     1. _____  _____
most famous.  For one thing (2) it was the first    2. _____  _____
widely used social network (3) a medium that al-    3. _____  _____
lows people to communicate almost instantaneously
and to share pictures (4) videos and other infor-   4. _____  _____
mation.  It wasn't the only social network oper-
ating in those early years of the century (5) of    5. _____  _____
course (6) MySpace was another one.  But Facebook   6. _____  _____
drew early attention (7) mainly by its ease of      7. _____  _____
use.  It became very popular as a way for people,
known on Facebook as "friends(8)" to share things   8. _____  _____
about their lives with others over the Internet.
        Two of Facebook's co-founders (9) Mark Zuck- 9. _____  _____
erberg and Eduardo Saverin—were portrayed in the
2010 film The Social Network (10) which chronicled 10. _____  _____
the rise of the social media platform.  The film
was nominated for an Oscar for best picture (11)   11. _____  _____
```

drawing attention to Zuckerberg and Saverin (12)   12. _____ _____
as well as to the social media site itself. The
film portrayed Zuckerberg (13) as an insecure cod-   13. _____ _____
ing whiz who first created a social network for
Harvard, where he went to college. The first site
was a platform that allowed users to compare the
attractiveness of students (14) in fact (15) the   14. _____ _____
site nearly got Zuckerberg kicked out of school.   15. _____ _____
But that prank gave way to what Zuckerberg orig-
inally called The Facebook (16) an early version   16. _____ _____
of Facebook that was adopted by several colleges.
     On May 18, 2012 (17) Facebook held its ini-   17. _____ _____
tial public offering (18) a financing mechanism in   18. _____ _____
which companies sell shares to the general public
for the first time. It was the biggest IPO in Internet history (19) raising more than $104 bil-   19. _____ _____
lion. By the fall of that year (20) the company   20. _____ _____
had one billion active users. Since then (21) it   21. _____ _____
has broadened its reach by purchasing the follow-
ing companies (22) Branch Media, Oclulus VR and   22. _____ _____
WhatsApp.
     Facebook has also begun offering several
privacy tools (23) one of them is an anonymous   23. _____ _____
login (24) that allows users to use apps without
revealing personal information.   24. _____ _____

Note: For some sentences, more than one answer is possible. Number 7, for instance, could be a comma or a dash, though a dash would serve to emphasize the extension "mainly by its ease of use." Numbers 18 and 19 could also, plausibly, be commas or dashes—depending on whether the student wants to emphasize the material in the extensions.

Name _____ Date _____

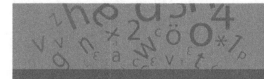
SUBORDINATION

A. Main Part only

B. Introduction and Main Part

C. Interruption and Main Part

D. Extension and Main Part

E. Intro., Inter., MP

F. Intro., Ext., MP

G. Inter., Ext., MP

H. Intro., Inter., Ext., MP

PARALLELISM

A. No parallelism

B. Compound

C. Series

D. Compound & Series

Directions: Place the appropriate letter in the blanks on the answer sheet provided on page 45 or on a similar answer sheet.

---

(1) The National Basketball Association was created in 1949 when its forerunner, the Basketball Association of America, bought and took over its rival league—the National Basketball League. (2) At that time, the league had 17 franchises. (3) However, by the 1953–54 season, just eight franchises remained: the Knicks, Celtics, Warriors, Lakers, Royals (later Kings), Pistons, Hawks and Nationals (later 76ers).

(4) Notably, all of those teams were located in cities in the eastern part of the United States. (5) In an era when trains and buses were the easiest way to travel, that made sense. (6) Those franchises formed the foundation of the league and are still active today. (7) Some have moved to other cities, notably the Lakers—who started in Minneapolis in 1947 before relocating to Los Angeles in 1960.

(8) The League has expanded greatly since those early days. (9) Today, the NBA consists of 30 teams—15 in the Western Conference and 15 in the Eastern Conference—that are located in every region of the country. (10) (One team is located in Canada). (11) The most recent city to get a franchise is Oklahoma City, which got a team in 2008 when the Seattle SuperSonics decided to relocate.

---

(12) One reason the league has been able to expand is obvious: money generated by television. (13) During the 2012-2013, the NBA generated approximately $5 billion in television revenue—an amount that was split between the teams. (14) With that kind of money and exposure, smaller market teams are able to at least compete when it comes to signing free agents, retaining star players and attracting top coaches—though they are still at a disadvantage. (15) Big market teams still have more money to spend. (16) But the revenue sharing allows teams in smaller cities—Minneapolis, Cleveland and Oklahoma City, for instance—to have viable and relevant franchises.

(17) It's unlikely that the NBA will expand any time soon in the United States. (18) According to one executive, the market is saturated. (19) But that doesn't mean the league couldn't expand elsewhere—including other countries besides Canada. (20) For several seasons, the NBA has been holding regular season games—that have been well attended—in Mexico City. (21) The league played its first regular season game in another country in 1990—in Tokyo, Japan. (22) The NBA has also played exhibition games in several other countries, including China, Israel and Italy.

(23) Indeed, with the popularity of basketball growing around the world, it might not be long before the NBA expands into another country. (24) That would only make sense, considering the success of a league that dates back to 1949.

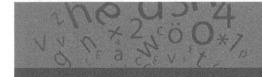

Practice test A-I

(Part 2)

PUNCTUATION MARK USED:

  A. Comma

  B. Semicolon

  C. Colon

  D. Dash

  E. Generally no punctuation needed

WHY PUNCTUATION MARK IS NEEDED:

  A. To set off introduction

  B. To set off interruption

  C. To set off extension

  D. To separate parts of a series

  E. To separate independent clauses [sentences]

  F. None [for E above]

Directions: Place the appropriate letters in the blanks on the answer sheet provided on page 45 or on a similar answer sheet.

> In the history of the National Basketball Association (1) three franchises have developed what might be considered dynasties.
> These three include the Lakers—a team that has been located in Minneapolis and Los Angeles (2) the Boston Celtics and the Chicago Bulls.
> The Minneapolis Lakers were the first dynasty in the NBA. The team won its first championship in the BAA (3) the Basketball Association of America—in 1949. The BAA was the forerunner to the NBA (4) which began the following year. After that BAA title (5) Minnesota won four championships in the NBA between 1950 and 1954. The Lakers moved to Los Angeles in 1960 (6) winning five titles in the 1980s with Magic Johnson at point guard and another five after that (7) most recently in 2010.
> Another dynasty (8) was created by the Celtics teams of the 1950s and 1960s. Led by the great center Bill Russell (9) Boston won eleven championships between 1957 and 1969. Red Auerbach was the coach for

most of those teams.   The Celtics won another six titles after that (10) most recently in 2008.

Finally (11) no list of NBA dynasties would be complete without the Chicago Bulls.   Led by the dynamic Michael Jordan (12) considered by some to be the best basketball player of all time (13) the Bulls won six titles between 1991 and 1998.

That's not to say (14) that other dynasties aren't possible. The Miami Heat—led by superstar LeBron James (15) won back-to-back titles in 2012 and 2013.   But even that story suggests (16) that dynasties just don't happen anywhere.   James left a city in the Midwest (17) Cleveland, where he didn't think he could win a championship and joined fellow stars Dwayne Wade and Chris Bosch in Miami.   The Heat was able to afford all three players (18) not every franchise is able to do that.   Consequently (19) the Heat made it to three consecutive NBA finals (20) winning championships in 2012 and 2013.

So (21) yes, dynasties are possible in the NBA.   But they are unlikely.   Most teams that become one have three things (22) money (23) location (24) and history.

| Name _____ | | Name _____ | |
| Date _____ | | Date _____ | |

Test No. _____ Score _____
(For Practice Test A II)

Test No. _____ Score _____
(For Practice Test A-I)

Part 1		Part 2		Part 1		Part 2	
Sub.	Para.	Punct.	Why?	Sub.	Para.	Punct.	Why?
1___	1___	1___	1___	1___	1___	1___	1___
2___	2___	2___	2___	2___	2___	2___	2___
3___	3___	3___	3___	3___	3___	3___	3___
4___	4___	4___	4___	4___	4___	4___	4___
5___	5___	5___	5___	5___	5___	5___	5___
6___	6___	6___	6___	6___	6___	6___	6___
7___	7___	7___	7___	7___	7___	7___	7___
8___	8___	8___	8___	8___	8___	8___	8___
9___	9___	9___	9___	9___	9___	9___	9___
10___	10___	10___	10___	10___	10___	10___	10___
11___	11___	11___	11___	11___	11___	11___	11___
12___	12___	12___	12___	12___	12___	12___	12___
13___	13___	13___	13___	13___	13___	13___	13___
14___	14___	14___	14___	14___	14___	14___	14___
15___	15___	15___	15___	15___	15___	15___	15___
16___	16___	16___	16___	16___	16___	16___	16___
17___	17___	17___	17___	17___	17___	17___	17___
18___	18___	18___	18___	18___	18___	18___	18___
19___	19___	19___	19___	19___	19___	19___	19___
20___	20___	20___	20___	20___	20___	20___	20___
21___	21___	21___	21___	21___	21___	21___	21___
22___	22___	22___	22___	22___	22___	22___	22___
23___	23___	23___	23___	23___	23___	23___	23___
24___	24___	24___	24___	24___	24___	24___	24___

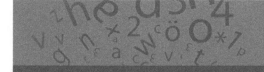

Practice test A-II
(Part 1)

SUBORDINATION

A. Main Part only

B. Introduction and Main Part

C. Interruption and Main Part

D. Extension and Main Part

E. Intro., Inter., MP

F. Intro., Ext., MP

G. Inter., Ext., MP

H. Intro., Inter., Ext., MP

PARALLELISM

A. No parallelism

B. Compound

C. Series

D. Compound & Series

Directions: Place the appropriate letter in the blanks on the answer sheet provided on page 45 or on a similar answer sheet.

---

(1) The space program is one of the crown jewels of innovation and engineering in the United States. (2) Countless space flights have broadened the world's view of the universe and led to spinoff technologies that have improved people's lives.

(3) The U.S. space program, however, has been far from flawless. (4) Two Space Shuttle flights ended in tragedy: the Challenger flight in 1986 and the Columbia flight in 2003. (5) Moreover, in the early days of the space program, the Gemini 8 and Apollo 13 space flights barely avoided disaster.

(6) The Challenger exploded on January 28, 1986, killing the entire crew. (7) The shuttle exploded over the Atlantic Ocean just 73 seconds after lifting off from Cape Canaveral, Florida, while a national television audience watched. (8) Seven people were killed, including Christa McAuliffe, who would have been the first teacher in space, and Ronald McNair, one of the country's first African-American astronauts. (9) An investigation showed that an O-ring seal in a solid rocket booster failed at liftoff, leading to the explosion.

(10) Seventeen years later, on February 1, 2003, the Columbia broke up over Texas and Louisiana upon re-entering the Earth's atmo-

---

sphere. (11) Like the Challenger, the Columbia had a crew of seven—and all seven died in the mishap. (12) An investigation revealed that the Columbia—which was on its 28th mission—was damaged when a piece of foam insulation broke off from an external tank and struck the left wing. (13) That allowed hot atmospheric gases to penetrate the internal wing structure, which led to the break-up of the shuttle.

(14) The first U.S. emergency in space involved the Gemini 8 flight—on March 16, 1966. (15) The two crew members on board, Neil Armstrong and David Scott, were practicing docking with a target vehicle when a steering jet malfunctioned—throwing the craft into violent rolls. (16) NASA officials said that—before the craft could be brought under control—the crew sustained forces up to 4Gs—a force considered dangerous is space.

(17) The other close call during the early days of space exploration happened on the ill-fated Apollo 13 flight. (18) Even though the three crewmen—James Lovell, Fred Haise and John Swigert—were not injured, their chances of getting back to earth safely were not very good. (19) About 55 hours into the flight, an oxygen tank on the spacecraft exploded. With such a crucial power source destroyed, the crew—merely to survive—had to use energy from the LM, the lunar module. (20) By using back-up systems, the crew coaxed the crippled craft around the moon and headed for home, managing a fairly normal splashdown.

(21) People will long remember the Columbia and Challenger space shuttle disasters and, to a lesser extent, the Gemini 8 and Apollo 13 missions that nearly ended in disaster. (22) And they should. (23) But those who follow the space program know that, on the whole, journeys into space have been safe. (24) Most missions have been pulled off successfully.

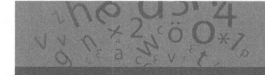

Practice test A-II

(Part 2)

PUNCTUATION MARK USED:

A. Comma

B. Semicolon

C. Colon

D. Dash

E. Generally no punctuation needed

WHY PUNCTUATION MARK IS NEEDED:

A. To set off introduction

B. To set off interruption

C. To set off extension

D. To separate parts of a series

E. To separate independent clauses [sentences]

F. None [for E above]

Directions: Place the appropriate letters in the blanks on the answer sheet provided on page 45 or on a similar answer sheet.

When the U.S. began its space program (1) most of the work was done at one location on Florida's coast: Cape Kennedy (2) a launch operation center. In a few years, much work on the space program was (3) however (4) being done in three other locations (5) at Huntsville (6) Alabama (7) Cleveland (8) Ohio (9) and Houston (10) Texas. In Houston, the government has the Lyndon B. Johnson Space Center (11) in Huntsville, it has the Marshall Space Flight Center. Both centers employ thousands of skilled workers: engineers (12) computer technicians (13) and craftsmen of all types.

By the mid-1960s, the aerospace industry employed more than 700,000 workers (14) and exceeded $15 billion in sales. (Note: Number 14 does not mark the beginning of an extension).

About 10,000 U.S. firms—located primarily along the west coast (15) the east coast and the gulf coast (16) worked on aerospace projects in the early days of space exploration.

The National Aeronautics and Space Administration (NASA) directs

---

the main national space activities (17) selects space programs (18) and manages the research and development of space craft and launch vehicles. Major space projects (19) such as Mercury (20) Gemini (21) and Apollo (22) were directed by NASA officials.

The U.S. Department of Defense uses space vehicles for military reconnaissance (23) the Agriculture Department uses space satellites for crop monitoring. One of the most spectacular uses of satellites is in the area of communications. TV signals (24) and telephone calls circle the globe in seconds.

WRITING INSIGHTS: Discovering the Keys to Structure and Content

Insight #3:

Usage Problems

Many student writers struggle with problems of usage—problems that basically involve structure, such as faulty agreement, run-ons and fragments. So another important insight that students of writing must acquire is an awareness of generally accepted conventions of usage—rules, if you like, for structure and word usage generally identified in most publisher's stylebooks.

INSIGHT #3: *Sentence Structure*: Writers follow conventions of usage (rules, if you like) that are followed by publishers and editors of newspapers and magazines, news Web sites and books.

Certain writing practices have evolved over the years that professional writers are required to follow. Publishers and editors follow stylebooks on usage that have become more and more uniform.

Students should become familiar with the usage errors that often occur in themes and papers. The following information and exercises should help them avoid many of these errors in their writing. In other words, the exercises will help them to become conscious of such errors in the sentences they write or read.

USAGE PROBLEMS—STRUCTURE

Just as an understanding of sentence structure—subordination and coordination—can help one understand punctuation, it can also help one understand usage problems, as well. Many of the errors in usage can be understood and eliminated by seeing how faulty structure often causes usage errors.

Some of the most frequent sentence errors in usage—such as fragmentary sentences and faulty parallelism, for instance—often result from a lack of sentence sense, from a lack of awareness of the subordination and coordination in sentences.

Listed below are the usage errors most frequently made:

A. FAULTY AGREEMENT [AG]

Faulty Subject-Verb: One error in usage frequently occurs because the writer is unaware of interruptions: choosing a verb that is not appropriate for the subject. Some texts call such an error "lack of agreement." The verb does not "agree" with the subject.

Example: U.S. astronauts, especially those who have been on many space shuttle missions, very often <u>receives</u> lucrative offers to speak about their experiences.

Often, when there is a long interruption, the writer forgets what the subject of the sentence is and picks a verb that is not appropriate.

An awareness of subordination—especially of interruptions—can help the student writer avoid faulty subject-verb combinations.

Faulty Pronoun Agreement: When a pronoun does not agree with its antecedent—the word to which it refers—it is considered unacceptable usage.

Example: Every student in the class completed <u>their</u> project on time.

Example: A number of players paid <u>his</u> own plane fare to attend the football game.

<u>Every student</u> is singular and the pronoun referring to it needs to be singular—<u>his</u>. <u>A number</u> is plural; the pronoun needs to be plural—<u>their</u>.

Faulty Word or Phrase Agreement: Words and phrases must agree with other words and phrases in the sentence that they repeat or relate to.

Example: U.S. astronauts, <u>a country that helped build the space station</u>, made significant discoveries in space.

The interruption—"a country that helped build the space station"—does not agree, in a sense, with astronauts. Phrases in that position either repeat the noun before them or relate logically in some way to them. This one does neither. It does not agree with the word it is supposed to relate to.

B. RUN-ON OR COMMA SPLICE [RNN]

Run-ons: A run-on sentence is also considered a serious error in usage. It is a group of words that is more than a sentence. The writer does not place appropriate punctuation where the sentence should end—a period, a semicolon or a colon. Again, awareness of structure can help the student avoid writing a run-on sentence.

Example: The Russians were the first to orbit a man in <u>space they</u> were also the first to orbit a woman in space.

The sentence should stop after space. Students of writing must somehow acquire enough sentence sense to recognize the main parts and subordinate elements of all sentences they write—where they begin, where they end.

Comma Splice: If a comma is used where the sentence ends, where a semicolon or a period should be used, it is a specific type of run-on sentence—often called a comma splice.

C. CORRECT   In the exercises that follow, the letter C will be used as an answer when sentences are correct.

D. DISTORTION [DIS]

Distorted Sentences: Distortion in sentences often occurs because the writers are not aware of the structure of the sentences they are writing—not aware of its main part, nor of its subordination and coordination.

Example: Some important discoveries in space have been made on experimental flights, originally planned perhaps for some other goal, <u>make invaluable contributions to space technology</u>.

The last element of the sentence—"make invaluable contributions to space technology"—does not fit with the rest of the sentence.

Note: The word distortion is generally used to label sentences that seem to be "a hopeless mess"—sentences in which the usual order has gone berserk. However, a flawed sentence should not be labeled "a distortion" if it has a faulty agreement, is a run-on or a comma splice, has faulty parallelism, is a fragment, has faulty modification or no clear pronoun reference. In other words, if the sentence's error cannot be identified, it should be called a distortion.

E. FAULTY PARALLELISM [PL]

Faulty Parallelism: A sentence with faulty parallelism has a faulty compound or series. Usually the error is the result of having different grammatical elements joined with and or some other coordinate conjunction or having different grammatical elements placed in a series.

Example: The early unmanned space flights were made primarily <u>to test computer control systems </u>and <u>collecting data about atmospheric conditions in space</u>.

Changing <u>collecting</u> to <u>to collect</u> would make the two elements parallel—grammatically alike, coordinated.

Example: A space flight requires close coordination of three separate units: a launch complex, a control center and <u>retrieving the space vehicle</u>.

Complex and center are nouns that identify definite organizations in the space program. The third unit should be identified with a similar noun—not one that identifies an activity or an organization. An expression such as <u>a retrieving task force</u> would be parallel (coordinated) with the other two.

An awareness of coordination—of compounds and series—will enable a writer to avoid faulty parallelism.

F. Fragment [F]

Fragments: A fragment is considered a serious writing error. It is treating part of a sentence—often an introduction or an extension—as though it were a sentence.

Example: <u>When the Russians took the lead in space exploration with the launching of Sputnik I.</u> The United States began an intensive rocket development program. <u>Designed primarily to facilitate eventual moon landings.</u>

Note: Most stylebooks and editors accept fragments in which essential elements are clearly understood. Example: He thought I was a thief. How absurd! (it was to think I was a thief). Or: What went wrong? <u>Plenty</u>. (of things went wrong.)

G. FAULTY MODIFICATION [MD]

Most grammar tests point to the following three faulty modifiers as the ones most frequently appearing on student papers:

Misplaced Modifiers: In most sentences, modifiers—adjectives and adverbs, both words and phrases—are placed either immediately before or after the words they modify. Often when they are not so placed, they modify some other word—usually resulting in unintended confusion or humor.

Example: John found a dog with a collar <u>named Snooper</u>. [recast sentence so <u>named Snooper</u> follows <u>dog</u>]

Example: Harry almost ate half of the pie. [<u>almost</u> modifies <u>half</u>, not <u>ate</u>] Harry ate almost half of the pie.

Squinting Modifiers: Some modifiers could relate to several words in the sentence and it is not clear what the writer intended.

Example: The speaker said last year the schools needed money. [<u>last year</u> could modify <u>said</u> or <u>needed</u>]

Example: His coach told him <u>frequently</u> to work out. [<u>frequently</u> could modify <u>told</u> or <u>to work out</u>]

Dangling Modifiers: Introductory modifiers that do not appropriately relate to the subject of the sentence are referred to in most grammar texts as dangling modifiers.

Example: To earn money for the trip, candy had to be sold at each game. [candy can not earn money nor take a trip; students can] To earn money for the trip, students had to sell candy at every game. [subject must relate logically to the introductory modifier]

Example: Before traveling to the moon, the United States had to develop new computers. [the United States can't travel to the moon]

Example: To improve relations with the Arab countries, ships carrying oil had to be allowed to use the canal. [ships are not interested in, nor capable of, improving relations with Arab countries]

H. NO CLEAR PRONOUN REFERENCE [RF]

Pronouns must have a clear antecedent (referent). If there is no noun—explicit or implied, in the sentence or previous sentences—to which the pronoun can clearly refer, the sentence is unacceptable.

Example: When Rhodesia declared its independence from England, they place an embargo on its products

The sentence does not have a noun to which the plural they can refer. They cannot refer to singular Rhodesia or England. To correct such an error, they could be changed to the United States, for instance, or some other noun. Its, the other pronoun in the sentence, clearly refers to Rhodesia.

Example: In a recent article on Africa, it shows how South Africa is improving its image in the West.

It does not have an antecedent; change it shows to a writer notes, an author explains, etc. Its clearly refers to South Africa.

Example: The country has vast resources of oil, but this is not publicized. [This what? this asset? this advantage? supply a noun for clarity]

The following exercises deal with errors in usage that students often make because they are not conscious of subordination and coordination in sentences. To avoid such errors, students of writing must develop an awareness of, some sensitivity to, the introductions, interruptions, extensions and parallel elements that it is possible for writers to use in sentences. From this awareness of sentence structure, the student writer should be able to write sentences that read well and should be able to use subordination and coordination appropriately.

Exercise #13:

Usage

USAGE:

A. Faulty Agreement

B. Run-on or Comma Splice

C. Correct

D. Distortion

E. Faulty Parallelism

F. Fragment

G. Faulty Modification

H. No Clear Pronoun Reference

Directions: Pick the letter above that most appropriately identifies the usage error in the sentence.

1. The life-support system includes—oxygen, food and water—are carried in stainless steel tanks.   1. _____

2. The Russians were the first to place an artificial satellite—Sputnik I—in space; the first to place a man—Yuri Gagarin—in space; and also placed the first woman in space: Valentina Tereshkova.   2. _____

3. When the Russians first launched their Sputniks into outer space to the amazement of the whole world, including the U.S.   3. _____

4. Inside an Apollo lunar module, the ground control center maintains constant communication with the astronauts.   4. _____

5. Russia, as well as the United States, have launched several communication satellites.   5. _____

6. Russia was the first nation to put a man into space the United States was the first nation to put a man on the moon.   6. _____

7. To insure accurate course determination, they use mini computers.   7. _____

8. Most astronauts are officers in some branch of the military; a few are civilians attached to U.S. space agencies.   8. _____

9. In Russian, especially during the '60s, conducted valuable experiments in space rescue operations.

9. _____

10. Russia, in the early 1960s, sought to lead the world in space probes, to excel in satellite production, the first to place a man in space and to surpass the U.S. in space communication systems.˙ (not D).

10. _____

11. Astronauts and cosmonauts who have landed on the moon—making extremely significant contributions to technology. (not D).

11. _____

12. Alan B. Shepard, Jr., who made the first U.S. space flight, also made a lunar landing, January 31, 1971.

12. _____

13. Russia made its first manned orbital flight on April 12, 1961, the U.S. did not make its first manned orbital flight until February 20, 1962.

13. _____

14. The Apollo command module, a mission that carried men to the moon, had several back-up control systems.

14. _____

15. Russia has two very celebrated space heroes. Yuri Gagarin, the first man to orbit the earth, and Valentina Tereshkova, the first woman to orbit the earth.

15. _____

16. Space probes, especially those that go beyond the gravitational force of the moon, advances man's knowledge of the universe.

16. _____

17. The Russians had the lead in the space race during the late 1950s and early 60s the U.S., however, definitely pulled ahead in the late '60s.

17. _____

18. In a recent article, it shows that in the late 50s the Russians led the U.S. in space exploration.

18. _____

19. The Russians, however, only reveal information about their space successes; they seldom tell the world about their failures.

19. _____

20. The Russian space agency, which trained the first cosmonauts, deserve a great deal of credit for early space discoveries.

20. _____

21. The U.S. space agency, which discovered the mysterious Van Allen radiation belts that astronauts must understand.

21. _____

22. Circling the moon, the Houston Space Center was careful to pick a flat area on which to land.

22. _____

23. At the Apollo, spaceport on Cape Kennedy, are carried on barges and crawlers to the launch pad.

23. _____

24. Space technology will enable man to travel to other planets, to build better communication satellites and probing space for new data on the universe. (not D).

24. _____

25. The U.S. Space Agency, developed and promoted by both Eisenhower and Kennedy, controls all aspects of space missions.

25. _____

Exercise #14:

Usage

USAGE:

A. Faulty Agreement

B. Run-on or Comma Splice

C. Correct

D. Distortion

E. Faulty Parallelism

F. Fragment

G. Faulty Modification

H. No Clear Pronoun Reference

Directions: Pick the letter above that most appropriately identifies the usage error in the sentence.

1. Africa not long ago was called—the Dark Continent—
    is still difficult to get information about many
    parts of the interior.   1. _____

2. To promote tourism in Africa, tigers provide big-game
    hunting for many American and European sportsmen.   2. _____

3. African countries export nearly three fourths
    of the world's palm oil, about one third of the
    world's peanuts and sisal is exported, too—almost
    two-thirds of the world's supply. (not D).   3. _____

4. In some African countries, one can only hunt during
    certain seasons, and then only in certain restrict-
    ed areas.   4. _____

5. Two powerful African countries have black majori-
    ties ruled by white minorities. South Africa and
    Rhodesia, both of which have many more black citi-
    zens than white.   5. _____

6. Most African people, especially countries that have
    recently gained independence, support the idea of
    pan-Africanism.   6. _____

7. Tanzania's Nyerere, whose experiments with social-
    ism draw much attention through Africa.   7. _____

8. In much of Africa, they lack modern industrial development.

9. Many African countries have—rich natural resources—do not have enough financial resources.

10. Zaire's Mobutu, a strongman who sees his nation as a leader toward African unity.

11. Strong national movements force European colonial powers to grant independence to many of their African possessions, six countries gained their independence during the 1950s.

12. African farmers grow most of the world's supply of—cocoa, palm oil, peanuts and sisal—such as ebony and mahogany. (not A).

13. The price of coffee and tea, two of African's principal exports, remain fairly high.

14. Most African nations have joined regional organizations—a people who have a history of unity and cooperation.

15. Many African countries have rich natural resources, only a few, however, have the financial means with which to develop them thoroughly.

16. In the 1960s, the Nigerians were embroiled in a civil war, in the early 1970s, however, they resolved their differences.

17. When African nations began their drive for independence from European nations.

18. To thousands of tourists visit Africa to make—trips to the world's longest river.

19. Most African farmers work their land in the old-fashioned ways of their ancestors.

20. Flying over the vast deserts and endless jungles, Africa is a continent that has immense potential—primarily because of its abundant natural resources.

21. In 1960, Niger received its independence; in 1965, Rhodesia declared itself independent.

22. Diamonds used in industry come from Angola, Ghana, Tanzania and ore rich in other minerals. (not D)

23. Africa, the second largest continent, is the scene of a great political revolution, as recently as 1950, only four African countries were independent.

24. The government of Kenya passed laws against hunting animals that were ridiculous.

25. To exploit their natural resources, the African nations have invited other nations to invest in its industries, have joined the world bank, have formed trade alliances and have attempted to stabilize its economy.

8. _____

9. _____

10. _____

11. _____

12. _____

13. _____

14. _____

15. _____

16. _____

17. _____

18. _____

19. _____

20. _____

21. _____

22. _____

23. _____

24. _____

25. _____

Aside from errors in the use of subordinate and coordinate elements, students often make mistakes in their choice of words—especially in instances where there are several similar words to choose from.

To eliminate most such errors from their papers, students of writing should do well to familiarize themselves with the following eight areas in which errors in the choice of words often occur.

A. WRONG HOMONYM [HOM]

Wrong Homonym: A few words in English are pronounced the same but are spelled differently and have different meanings and uses: for instance, **there and their; sight, site and cite**. Also, a few words are pronounced and spelled almost in the same way: for instance, **moral and morale; quite, quiet and quit**.

Students must be careful to use the correct form when they use such words. Some other examples include **council, counsel, consul; die, dye; fair, fare; faze, phase; hear, here; hole, whole; new, knew; no, know; led, lead; plain, plane; profit, prophet; roll, role; sore, soar; than, then; weak, week**; etc.

Unless students are careful in their choices of words, they will often make the error of using a word that merely sounds like, or is spelling approximately like, the word that should be used. The error is often called a malapropism.

Example: The president of the club <u>proceeded</u> his resignation speech with a warning about financial trouble ahead for the organization. [<u>preceded</u> is the correct word]

Example: The <u>country's</u> of Africa were encouraged to join the alliance. [<u>countries</u> is the correct word]

Example: The lunar craft has <u>it's</u> own power supply. [<u>its</u> is the correct word]

Example: When <u>its</u> cold outside, cars need special care. [<u>it's</u> is correct]

B. TRITE EXPRESSION [TRI]

Avoid trite, overused expressions that have become clichés—such as beat a hasty retreat, believe it or not, better late than never, couldn't care less, crying shame, few and far between, first and foremost, in the last analysis, it stands to reason, last but not least, let's face it, never ending, sneaking suspicion, tender mercies, truth is stranger than fiction, etc.

Also, **avoid trite overused figures of speech—such as the following similies** (figures of comparison that use <u>like</u> or <u>as</u>: pretty as a picture, brave as a lion, run like a deer, sly as a fox, spreading like wildfire, white as snow, quick as a wink, etc.).

Also **avoid trite metaphors** (figures of comparison that say something is what it cannot be, or does something it cannot do, for the sake of comparison): in the lap of luxury, bolt out of the blue, burn the midnight oil, dire straits, the last straw, rear its ugly head, rude awakening, a shot in the arm, sink or swim, strike while the iron is hot, the straight and narrow, up in arms, etc.

C. CORRECT

D. REDUNDANT [RED]

Avoid unnecessary repetition of key words in sentences or adjoining sentences.

Example: The <u>problem</u> of providing enough classrooms is this country's major <u>problem</u>.

Example: <u>Congress</u> quickly approved the measure. <u>Congress</u> generally looks with favor on such action. [<u>It</u> would avoid unnecessary repetition]

There is a fine line between what is necessary and unnecessary repetition. But if it does not sound right, choose a pronoun or a synonym or a synonymous phrase.

E. SUPERFLUOUS [SUP]

Avoid unnecessary repetition of ideas and information in sentences or adjoining sentences. (Note that redundancy involves sound—repetition of the same sound, the same word: superfluous does not relate to sound.)

Example: In the next ten years, Africa will <u>in the future</u> be basically <u>and primarily</u> interested in developing its natural resources <u>and mineral wealth</u>.

Example: Teachers agree <u>these days with the concept</u> that the marking system used in most schools should be changed.

The same words are not repeated, but the same ideas and information are repeated unnecessarily.

F. UNIDIOMATIC [IDI]

Unidiomatic Expressions: Every language, over the years, acquires idioms—usages and expressions that are preferred to—thought to be more acceptable than—similar expressions for no logical reason other than "that is the way it is used (said) by educated people."

Example: The final examination was different <u>than</u> the mid-semester. [from is considered idiomatic—correct]

Following are a few examples of idiomatic and unidiomatic expressions:

Idiomatic [acceptable]		unidiomatic [unacceptable]
*fewer people	not	less people
*a number of people	not	amount of people
accompanied by Harry	not	accompanied with Harry
abhorrent to an idea	not	abhorrent of an idea
take advantage of him	not	take advantage over him
pertinent to the argument	not	pertinent with the argument
similar to mine	not	similar with mine
plea bargaining is a procedure	not	plea bargaining is when
baseball is a game	not	baseball is where
a violation of our standards	not	a violation to our standards
incurred by World War II	not	incurred from World War II

*the words fewer and a number should be used for things one can count; less and amount, for things one cannot count.

G. GRAMMATICAL ERROR [GR]

Wrong Pronoun Case (form): Pronouns in English are used in one form when they are used as subjects or subjective complements of the sentence or clauses (sentences within the sentence). They are used in another form when they are used as objects of verbs or prepositions.

Example: They are the ones who received the money. [They and who are subjects; They is the subject of are in the sentence; who is the subject of received in the clause—a subordinate sentence within the sentence]

Example: We saw them—whom our classmates had elected as officers. [them and whom are objects; them is the object of the verb saw in the main part of the sentence; whom is the object of had elected in the clause—a subordinate sentence within the sentence]

Example: This is he. Who is your teacher? [he and who are subjective complements—predicate pronouns; therefore, the subject form is used]

Subject form: he, she, I, we, who, they and you. (sometimes called nominative form)

Object form: him, her, me, us, whom, them and you.

To be verbs: <u>am</u>, <u>are</u>, <u>is</u>, <u>was</u>, <u>were</u>, <u>be</u>, <u>being</u>, <u>have been</u>, etc. plus verbs that are often substituted for to be verbs—<u>become</u>, <u>seem</u>, <u>grow</u>, <u>appear</u>, <u>look</u>, <u>feel</u>, <u>smell</u>, <u>taste</u>, <u>remain</u>, <u>stay</u>, <u>prove</u>, <u>sound</u>, etc. (these verbs take subjective complements—predicate pronouns in subject form—rather than objects—in object form)

Wrong Pronoun Number: (singular, plural) (agreement) Students—because they have used the language so long—are familiar with singular and plural subjects and usually pick appropriate verbs to go with them—that agree with them. Occasionally, however, students make mistakes in keeping nouns and pronouns consistent in number (consistently plural or singular) throughout the sentence.

Example: A student must be careful when <u>they</u> choose <u>their</u> courses. [<u>they</u> and <u>their</u> are not the same number as <u>A student</u>; <u>they</u> and <u>their</u> are plural; <u>A student</u> is singular]

Wrong Adjective Adverb: Often students choose an adjective when they should use an adverb and vice versa.

Example: He plays <u>good</u>. [should be an adverb like <u>well</u> to modify verb plays]

Example: He did not follow the directions <u>careful</u>—as he was advised to do. [adverb <u>carefully</u> is needed to modify the verb follow]

Example: He feels <u>badly</u>. [should be adjective <u>bad</u> after linking verb <u>feels</u>; <u>feels</u> here equals <u>is</u> or some to be verb and should be followed by something that can be a subjective complement—like an adjective]

Remember! After to be verbs (listed under Wrong Pronoun Case above), adjectives, not adverbs, should be used. Adverbs cannot be subjective complements; adjectives can be.

Wrong Verb: As was noted previously in this chapter—under faulty subject-verb—the wrong verb is sometimes chosen when the writer is unaware of an interruption and chooses a verb that does not agree with the subject. In addition, there are troublesome verbs—such as lie and lay— and irregular verbs—such as sing, sang, sung—that can easily be use erroneously:

Some troublesome verbs:

These <u>must have objects</u>—

raise	raised	raised
set	set	set
lay	laid	laid

Example: He laid the book on the table. [correct—book is the object]

These <u>must not have objects</u>—

rise	rose	risen
sit	sat	sat
lie	lay	lain

Example: The dog lay on the sidewalk. [correct—no object]

Some irregular verbs:

swing	swung	swung	burst	burst	burst
hang	hung	hung [picture]	see	saw	seen
hang	hanged	hanged [executed]	take	took	taken
do	did	done	give	gave	given
swim	swam	swum			

Example: To improve its profit margin, the company has launched a public relations program and <u>went</u> to sales and promotion projects. [the verb form <u>went</u> does not go with <u>has</u> that is common to both <u>launched</u> and <u>went</u>; change to <u>gone</u>; <u>has gone</u> is correct.

Avoid double negatives, comparisons and connectives: Be careful to avoid using two conjunctions, for instance, when one is appropriate.

Double Negatives:	Students do<u>n't</u> want to buy <u>no</u> more books than they need. (two negative words; only one is needed)
Double Comparisons:	He will become <u>more</u> stronger if he exercises regularly. (<u>more</u> and <u>er</u> make the same comparison)
Double Conjunctions:	<u>But</u> he did not prove to be as versatile, <u>however</u>, as last year's pitcher. (both words make a transition; only one is needed)
Avoid Omissions: Wrong:	Mark will go <u>to with</u> Jim. (obvious omission of needed words between <u>to</u> and <u>with</u>.
Avoid:	The moon shot brought about many new <u>changes</u> in spite of predictions to the contrary. (changes in what?)

Avoid:	For years, Smokey the Bear, America's most famous <u>symbol</u>, has served the U.S. National Park Service loyally and effectively. (symbol of what?)
Avoid:	<u>This</u> was brought up later during the business meeting. (This what?)

H. INAPPROPRIATE EXPRESSION [INA]

Inappropriate Words: (weak words, slang, jargon, substandard words, etc.) Sometimes errors in usage result from the choice of inappropriate words—not merely the wrong use of appropriate, acceptable words—as is true in most categories above.

Some inappropriate words for most student papers are generally found in these areas:

<u>Weak words</u>: Some words are so general in meaning they are of little value in writing—such words as <u>nice</u>, <u>terrific</u>, <u>wonderful</u>, <u>splendid</u>, etc.

<u>Slang</u>: Slang expressions are not generally considered acceptable in student papers—unless they are used to depict a character's speech.

Example: The Supreme Court decision <u>clobbered</u> the practice of giving rebates to large companies. [<u>stopped</u> or <u>curtailed</u> would be appropriate]

<u>Jargon</u>: Avoid words that are used exclusively by one group.

Example: The students <u>miced</u> the shafts and <u>trued</u> the bearings before reassembling the motor. [<u>measured</u> the shafts and <u>adjusted</u> the bearings would be more appropriate in student papers]

<u>Substandard Words</u> (illiteracies): <u>ain't</u>, <u>git</u>, <u>scairt</u>, <u>snuck</u>, <u>he learned me</u>, <u>tooken</u>, etc.
<u>Invented Words</u>: <u>irregardless</u>, <u>confliction</u>, <u>unrational</u>, etc.

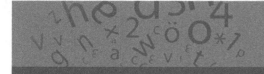

Exercise #15:

Usage (words)

A. Wrong Homonym [hom] [words have same or nearly same pronunciation]
B. Trite Expression [Tri] [clichés]
C. CORRECT
D. Redundant [red] [unnecessary repetition of the same word/words]
E. Superfluous [Sup] [unnecessary repetition of ideas or information]
F. Unidiomatic Expression [Idi]
G. Grammatical Error [Gra] [wrong pronoun, adjective, verb, etc; double negatives, prepositions, etc; lack of agreement, etc.]
H. Inappropriate Expression [Ina] [weak words, slang, jargon, substandard words, invented words, etc.]

Directions: Pick the letter above that most appropriately identifies the usage error in the sentence. [Each letter is used 2, 3, or 4 times.]

1. The students could not sell there textbooks back to the bookstore.

1. _____

2. My uncle gave Bill and I tickets to the all-star game.

2. _____

3. The members of the committee were quite surprised when they heard the president's testimony.

3. _____

4. When a student makes out his schedule, the student must be careful to indicate the course number.

4. _____

5. Nationalism began to rear its ugly head in new African nations.

5. _____

6. I think the summer months are the most enjoyable of the year.

6. _____

7. There were less education majors enrolled for winter quarter than there were for fall quarter.

7. _____

8. The team will go to the Orange Bowl—irregardless of its win-loss record.

8. _____

9. In labor relations, collective bargaining occurs when representatives of both labor and management work out new contractual agreements.

9. _____

10. There have been a number of conflictions in the Middle East over oil rights.

10. _____

11. The student counsel acted on the proposal at its last meeting.

11. _____

12. Many of the players paid his own way to the all-star game.

12. _____

13. The scholarship was given to Bill Stewart. Bill Stewart was selected as the outstanding athlete of the year.

13. _____

14. Most students feel badly about the arbitrary dropping of courses from the curriculum.

14. _____

15. A number of students who received scholarships were not required to take their final examinations.

15. _____

16. She was so adult about accepting responsibility for making the error and immediately corrected the error.

16. _____

17. A large amount of young people came to the rock concert held in the college's auditorium.

17. _____

18. It was them who determined which textbook should be used.

18. _____

19. Harry Brown, who was the coach's choice, would really burn the midnight oil.

19. _____

20. The amount of people who attended the soccer game surprised school officials.

20. _____

21. Both the faculty and the students have active rolls in determining curriculum.

21. _____

22. All during the meeting, the computer, that could have been used to clarify many points, sat along the wall unused.

22. _____

23. Unfortunately, the plot to oust the dictator was nipped in the bud.

23. _____

24. The punctuation mark most often used is the comma. The comma is used, for instance, to set apart all interruptions.

24. _____

25. I believe that every person on earth should have the chance to choose the kind of work or job he or she wants to do.

25. _____

Name _____ Date _____

Exercise #16:

Usage (words)

A. Wrong Homonym [hom] [words have same or nearly same pronunciation]
B. Trite Expression [Tri] [clichés]
C. CORRECT
D. Redundant [red] [unnecessary repetition of the same word/words]

E. Superfluous [Sup] [unnecessary repetition of ideas or information]
F. Unidiomatic Expression [Idi]
G. Grammatical Error [Gra] [wrong pronoun, adjective, verb, etc; double negatives, prepositions, etc; lack of agreement, etc.]
H. Inappropriate Expression [Ina] [weak words, slang, jargon, substandard words, invented words, etc.]

Directions: Pick the letter above that most appropriately identifies the usage error in the sentence. [Each letter is used 2, 3, or 4 times.]

1. The boys were suspended because they had snuck out. (not G)

1. _____

2. The secretary took the folder from the desk and lay the pamphlet down in its place.

2. _____

3. The president of the college was accompanied with the dean of students at the accreditation hearing.

3. _____

4. The directions were presented very explicit in class discussions about the assignment.

4. _____

5. Several company's refused to join the organization. (not G)

5. _____

6. The report was given to we who were on the committee.

6. _____

7. Television is where students acquire their sense of values and their images of society.

7. _____

8. The practice was a violation of board policy, accepted and ratified by the student senate.

8. _____

9. The members of the team new their chances of winning the conference were not very good.

   9. _____

10. A number of players paid their own plane fare to attend the bowl game.

   10. _____

11. India has had many tough breaks since she acquired her independence from England.

   11. _____

12. There folder lay unused on the table all during the conference.

   12. _____

13. The ambassador was such a sourpuss he was not well received in the diplomatic community.

   13. _____

14. We arose at the crack of dawn to pack our gear for the long hike.

   14. _____

15. The Red Cross helps out primarily in major disaster areas. The Red Cross relies primarily on contributions from individuals.

   15. _____

16. I think all eighteen-year olds, as far as I'm concerned, should be able to vote.

   16. _____

17. The democracies had to strike when the iron was hot.

   17. _____

18. Travel through space to the moon is, in some ways, dangerous and hazardous.

   18. _____

19. His new car is similar with the one he was using when he had the accident.

   19. _____

20. The committee presented a good report on the college's extracurricular policies.

   20. _____

21. The committee sure did a thorough investigation of all the evidence.

   21. _____

22. It is my belief that space travel can serve no useful purpose or can have no practical application.

   22. _____

23. Russia was quick to exploit its lead in the space race. Russia always uses whatever it can for propaganda purposes.

   23. _____

24. Russia's Sputniks hit the world like a bolt out of the blue.

   24. _____

25. The danger in space is the danger of rupturing the life-support system.

   25. _____

WRITING INSIGHTS: Discovering the Keys to Structure and Content

QUOTATION MARKS: **APOSTROPHES:**   **HYPHENS:**

Quotation marks are used, of course, around direct quotes and also around titles of selections that are a part of a book, newspaper, magazine, pamphlet, etc.—such as an article in a magazine or a poem in a book.

Most errors in the use of quotes appear to occur because they are often misplaced in relation to other punctuation marks. Remember!:

1. Commas and periods always go inside quotes (,"."")—even if in some situations it seems inappropriate, such as in a series of titles. Ex.: "Experimental People," "On Texas," "Skin In The Game," "Her Again" and "Berlin Nights" are all good articles on contemporary culture in the March 24, 2014, issue of *The New Yorker*, a leading magazine of reportage, commentary and fiction. (The commas after . . . Texas," and . . . Game," seem misplaced but they are not; it would be wrong, by most stylebooks, to have . . . Texas", and . . . Game",)

2. Semicolons, colons and dashes always go outside quotes ("; ": and "—)

3. Question marks and exclamation marks sometimes go inside, sometimes go outside quotes, depending on whether just the quote is a question (inside) or the quote plus additional material constitute the question (outside)

Example: Jim asked, "Did you pass the test?" [only the quote is a question; question mark is inside] Did the teacher say "Hand in your papers"? [whole sentence is a question; question mark is outside]

Direct Quotes: There are three strong conventions (practices) concerning quotes:

1. **Most direct quotes are complete sentences with a "he said" expression tacked on in the form of an introduction, interruption, or extension:**

Example: He said, "The United States should use more of its vast reserves of coal."

"The United States," he said, "should use more of its vast reserves of coal."

"The United States should us more of its vast reserves of coal," he said.

In the first example above, <u>he said</u> is an introduction; in the second, it is an interruption; and in the third, it is an extension. That interpretation squares with punctuation practices that have evolved and become very solid.

2. **Often direct quotes are preceded by more than a <u>he said</u> expression. Sometimes it is more of <u>he said [what]</u>:**

Example: He said our country should use another energy source: "The United States should use more of its vast reserves of coal."

Now the structure is different: the first part is the main part; the quotation is the extension. That interpretation squares with the use of the colon before the quote—another solid practice that has evolved.

3. **Often less than a complete sentence is quoted. Then the partial quote becomes a part of the main sentence and the <u>he said</u> generally becomes part of the main sentence as well:**

Example: He said our country "should use more of its vast reserves of coal."

<u>He said</u> in these sentences is not an introduction, interruption or an extension and is not set off with commas.

Note: Students are imaginative and resourceful enough to think of appropriate "he said" expressions for the quotes they use. Here are a few examples:

he said,	<u>Obama</u>, after much deliberation, <u>said</u>,
Obama noted,	<u>The prisoner</u> who had been apprehended <u>protested</u>,
she indicated,	<u>Tony Judt</u>, a famous Harvard professor of
they acknowledged,	European history, in a recent article on the UN <u>said</u>,
the senator emphasized,	(<u>he said</u> expressions are not always short; in the
John exclaimed,	first reference to a source, the complete name
*the student protested,	should be used along with necessary identifying
he quickly explained,	material, the title of the source should be given
*she vehemently complained,	and other relevant material is often used)

*Some verbs, like <u>protested</u> and <u>complained</u>, at times make complete statements without additional material and are followed by colons:

Example: He said, "The United States . . ." [he said what?] [something is needed]
          He protested: "The United States . . ." [he protested:] [<u>what</u> is not needed]

Note: **He protested, "The United States . . ." [<u>He protested</u> is an introduction and the quote is the main part of the sentence]**

           He protested: "The United States . . ." [<u>He protested</u> is the main part of the sentence and the quote is an extension]

These interpretations are the only ones possible in view of the punctuation practices that have evolved concerning quotes. They explain the use of the comma after <u>protested</u>—to set off the introduction; they explain the use of the colon after <u>protested</u>—before an extension.

Hyphens are used for two purposes: to create compound words and to separate words at the end of a line. Most errors in the use of hyphen seem to occur in these three situations:

1. **Be careful to divide words between syllables when they must be split at the end of a line. Use a dictionary to identify syllables when you are not sure how a word should be divided.**

2. **Do not use hyphens [-] where a dash [—] is needed. In longhand, be sure dashes are twice as long as hyphens.**

3. Do not fail to hyphenate common compound nouns: twenty-one, father-in-law. Be careful, too, to hyphenate compound adjectives that are generally coined and unusual: military-industrial complex, desk-top blotter. [Note the nouns modified—complex and blotter; awareness of the noun modified can help one spot the compound adjective]

Apostrophes are used for two purposes: to show possession and to indicate a contraction: the college's placement office (possessive), won't (contraction). Most errors in the use of the apostrophe seem to involve only two situations:

1. Remember! Its is possessive. This seems contradictory because other short possessives need the apostrophe: the boy's father, the car's windshield. But boy and car are nouns. It is a pronoun and its is the possessive form.

2. Remember! Country's is not plural; countries is. A word like country's needs a noun in front of it to modify, not a verb like is. Ex.: The country's armed forces were strong. [armed forces is the necessary noun following the possessive country's]

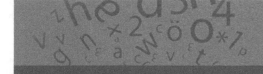

Practice test B-I

(Part 1)

PUNCTUATION MARKS:

A. Comma

B. Semicolon

C. Colon

D. Dash

E. Period

F. Quotation mark

G. Apostrophe

H. Hyphen

I. Question mark

J. Generally no punctuation needed

Directions: Place the appropriate letter in the blanks on the answer sheet provided on page 81 or on a similar answer sheet.

When space exploration began in the early 1950s(1)two countries, the United States and Russia(2)emerged as competitors. Each wanted to be the first nation to launch an artificial satellite, the first to make a manned orbital flight(3)the first to orbit the moon and the first to land on the moon. As it turned out, Russia led in the early stages of the raced and chalked up three impressive "firsts(4)(5)the first artificial satellite, October 4, 1957; the first manned orbital flight(6)April 12(7)1961(8)the first woman in space(9)June 10(10)1963.

Russia(11)s launching of the first artificial satellite, Sputnik I(12) took the United States by surprise. It clearly indicated that Russia had developed more powerful rocket(13)s than the U.S. had(14) it also indicated that Russia had made unusual advancements in it(15) s technological development. In the early 1960s, Russia continued to impress the world with it(16)s space spectaculars. On April 12, 1961, it sent the first man into orbital flight—Yuri Gagarin(17)on June 16, 1963(18) it sent the first woman into orbital flight(19)Valentina Tereshkova. It(20)s clear that the Russians dominated the early years of the space race. "Russia at first had more rocket power(21)(22) one

U.S. space expert lamented. "Russian space technology(23)(24)he added, "was geared for heavier payloads(25)(26)

If Russia was out front in the space race in the late '50s and
early '60s(27)the United States, in many ways(28)took the lead in the
late '60s. Starting in 1968, it, too(29)began chalking up some impressive "firsts(30)(31) the first lunar orbit, December 21, 1968(32)
the first lunar landing, July 16, 1969(33) the first Martian orbit, May
30, 1971.

The most spectacular "first" for the U.S.(34)of course(35)was
the lunar landing. Superior space(36)flight planning enabled the U.S.
to execute the landing earlier than most space(37)experts expected.
Three astronauts(38)Neil Armstrong(39)Edwin Aldrin and Michael Col-
lins(40)made the historic flight. Armstrong(41)the first man on the
moon(42)made the following now(43)famous statement as he stepped to
the moon(44)s surface from the LM(45) "One small step for man; one
giant step for mankind!" Later, another astronaut wistfully asked(46)
"Is this the extent of man(47)s travel(48)s into space(49)(50)

Practice test B-I

(Part 2)

USAGE:

A. Faulty Agreement

B. Run-on or Comma Splice

C. Correct

D. Distortion

E. Faulty Parallelism

F. Fragment

G. Faulty Modification

H. No Clear Pronoun Reference

Directions: Pick the letter above that most appropriately identifies the error in the sentence. (Each letter is used 2, 3 or 4 times). Use the answer sheet on page 81 or a similar answer sheet.

1. One of the most colorful countries in Europe is Spain, it has everything a tourist could possibly wish for.

2. The country has miles of white sand beaches for swimming, hundreds of mountain slopes for skiing and fishing lakes by the thousands.

3. Vacationers, primarily from Europe and the U.S., enjoys the famous resort areas along the Atlantic Coast.

4. The bathing beaches along—the Bay of Biscay—the famous resorts enjoy the vacationers.

5. When people first discovered Spain as a vacation land, with 1,400 castles and visit.

6. More than 3,000 years ago, they say the ancient Phoenicians set up colonies on the Spanish coast.

7. Later, the Carthaginians and the Romans, countries that were interested in establishing new colonies, invaded Spain.

8. After the fall of Rome, fierce German tribes swept into Spain from the north, destroyed most of the cities and most of the people were killed.

9. Coming over the mountains from the north, Spain was ravaged by barbarians.

10. After 1200, the Spanish people gradually expelled the Moors.

11. Christopher Columbus landed on the American continent and claimed it for Spain, soldiers and colonists followed him and sent back gold and jewels.

12. Spanish colonies in the new world were established to spread Christianity was the goal of the church.

13. By the 1500s, Spain had become the most powerful country in the world, gold and silver from the new world made Spain the richest country in Europe.

14. During the years that followed, however, wars with England and France brought Spain to the brink of financial disaster.

15. Spain lost most of her colonies the wars were too costly. (not D)

16. Despite advance in industry and technology in the rest of the world.

17. Citizens of Spain are either wealthy or poor are constantly frustrated by high unemployment and poverty.

18. Spain almost needs all the food it can produce for its own people.

19. The colorful bullfights, refined by the Moors, show the love Spanish people have for a spectacle that combines courage and elaborate ceremony.

20. Most of the people live in the coastal regions, a mild climate throughout the year.

21. Spain's leaders said last year they needed more exports.

22. When Spain sought to establish a democracy, a civil war that brought Franco to power for forty years. (not D)

23. Castille is a region famous for bullfights, for dances with castanets and most of the peasants play guitars.

24. A Spaniard, especially one from a remote area, is very proud of their musical heritage.

25. Because of changes in the Spanish government, they say Spain should remain a stable democracy in the decades after Franco's reign.

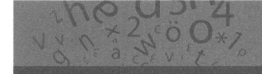

Practice test B-I

(Part 3)

USAGE (WORDS):

A. Wrong Homonym [hom] [words Have same or nearly same Pronunciation]
B. Trite expression [Tri] [clichés]
C. Correct
D. Redundant [red] [unnecessary Repetition of the same word/ words]

E. Superfluous [Sup] [unnecessary repetition of ideas or information]
F. Unidiomatic Expression [idi]
G. Grammatical Error [Gra] [wrong pronoun, adjective, adverb, verb, etc; double negatives, prepositions, etc; lack of agreement, etc.]
H. Inappropriate Expression [ina] [weak words, slang, jargon substandard words, etc.]

Directions: Pick the letter above that most appropriately identifies the error in the sentence. (Each letter is used 2, 3 or 4 times). Use the answer sheet on page 81 or a similar answer sheet.

1. Africa is a splendid country with a tremendous future.

2. Burundi, it is true, has very poor people in it's cities. (not G)

3. Africa is a continent that has more natural resources than any other continent.

4. African whites are generally gentlemen farmers, even though labor shortages have forced them too do much of their own work. (not G)

5. The accompanying music sounds oddly to a trained musician.

6. Much of the industry in the Malagasy Republic is socialistic and government owned.

7. Some African governments have had a difficult time making there governments work.

8. Abundant natural resources could make Africa a leading industrial area of the world. Abundant natural resources have created some problems in Africa.

9. African nations are faced with racial strife and problems arising from differences between blacks and whites.

10. Zambia's economy has for several years ben depressed by a very low growth rate.

11. For many of the new nations in Africa, self-government provided a rude awakening to international responsibilities.

12. Less people in Africa include red meat in their diet than in Europe or the United States.

13. In the next ten years, Africa will in the future be basically and primarily interested in developing its natural resources and mineral wealth.

14. Agriculture in Africa is different than farming in Europe or the United States.

15. Reevaluation of the U.S. dollar gave the economies of most African nationals a shot in the arm.

16. Egypt is an African nation that is extremely proud of their history.

17. In recent years, nationalism has begun to rear its ugly head in most of Africa.

18. Somalia is spending millions of dollars and a lot of money to start new industries.

19. The major problem in Africa is the problem of racial strife.

20. The Cameroon, formerly called the French Cameroon, has a great number of small farmers.

21. In some emerging African nations, socialism is spreading like wildfire.

22. Not so long ago, Africa was called the Dark Continent because much of it was unknown to Europeans.

23. The professor witnessed the signing of the treaty in Paris and seen the document years later in a museum.

24. The Belgian Congo is now called Zaire. The Belgian Congo is one of the richest nations in Africa.

25. Guinea is a great country with a terrific habitat for wild animals.

WRITING INSIGHTS: Discovering the Keys to Structure and Content

Name _____

Date _____

Test No. _____ Score _____
(For Practice Test B I)

Part 1	Part 2	Part 3
1._____ 26._____	1._____	1._____
2._____ 27._____	2._____	2._____
3._____ 28._____	3._____	3._____
4._____ 29._____	4._____	4._____
5._____ 30._____	5._____	5._____
6._____ 31._____	6._____	6._____
7._____ 32._____	7._____	7._____
8._____ 33._____	8._____	8._____
9._____ 34._____	9._____	9._____
10._____ 35._____	10._____	10._____
11._____ 36._____	11._____	11._____
12._____ 37._____	12._____	12._____
13._____ 38._____	13._____	13._____
14._____ 39._____	14._____	14._____
15._____ 40._____	15._____	15._____
16._____ 41._____	16._____	16._____
17._____ 42._____	17._____	17._____
18._____ 43._____	18._____	18._____
19._____ 44._____	19._____	19._____
20._____ 45._____	20._____	20._____
21._____ 46._____	21._____	21._____
22._____ 47._____	22._____	22._____
23._____ 48._____	23._____	23._____
24._____ 49._____	24._____	24._____
25._____ 50._____	25._____	25._____

Insight #4:

Thesis

In most pieces of writing, writers present a thesis and then proceed to defend (support) that thesis with detailed evidence. So another important **insight** that students of writing must acquire—insofar as content is concerned—is an awareness of the part that theses and the defense of theses play in writing.

INSIGHT #4: **Content:** Writing is basically presenting a conclusion (a judgment, opinion, position) and defending it with relevant, detailed evidence.

Note: The word conclusion is used here as it is used in logic: One concludes that a statement is true—based on evidence or other conclusions (premises). The word conclusion will not be used to mean the ending or summary of a piece of writing. The terms clincher, concluding statement, summary, etc., will be used for the closing statement of a portion of writing.

Below are the opening sentences of several news articles written by professional writers. These articles all begin with a conclusion (a judgment, opinion, position) the writer has come to about the subject and proceeds with a defense of that conclusion. Composition texts call this conclusion the thesis, and all good pieces of writing have one, clearly stated or implied. As we shall note later, they do not often begin the articles as in the following examples, but they almost always appear near the beginning of the article.

The New York Times, Jan. 8, 2014	**Associated Press, April 10, 2014**	**The New York Times, April 23, 1970**
WASHINGTON – For two years, President Obama has boasted that he accomplished what his predecessors had not. "I ended the war in Afghanistan," he has told audience after audience. <u>But a resurgence of Islamic militants in western Iraq has reminded the world that the war is anything but over.</u>	ST. PAUL, Minn. – <u>Minnesota workers earning the minimum wage will see yearly raises under a bill given final approval Thursday</u> that pushes the hourly rate to $9.50 by 2016 and enables automatic increases in the future.	NEW YORK – <u>There are two Lenins.</u> One is a real man, a shrewd, instinctive politician...

S+J=THESIS

Note how each thesis above—underlined—has a subject (S) and a judgment (J). Every good thesis has these two elements: **S and J**. Sometimes they are implied but they must be there.

In the first example, the **S** is <u>a resurgence of Islamic militants in western Iraq</u> and the **J** is that it <u>has reminded the world that the war is anything but over</u>. (Some journalists and military experts might argue that the war is over because U.S. troops have withdrawn, but this writer argues that it isn't and will defend this conclusion—this judgment, opinion, position or whatever synonym for conclusion one wants to use.)

In example 2, the **S** is <u>Minnesota workers earning the minimum wage</u> and the **J** is that they <u>will see yearly raises under a bill given final approval Thursday</u>. (This is a very safe conclusion, a factual statement—the kind that writers often use as theses for news stories or very objective accounts. The reader, of course, can expect details to follow that will defend, support, and warrant the statement). (See "More about theses" on page 108.)

In the last example, the **S** is <u>Lenin</u> and the **J** is that <u>there are two</u>. (Some people and writers might argue that there are three, four or just one Lenin, etc. This writer says there are two and will defend this conclusion—this judgment, opinion, position or whatever synonym or conclusion one wants to use.)

Writing Assignment 4-1

10-Sentence Theme

Write a ten-sentence theme, using one of the following subject areas: education, sports, politics or entertainment. Sentence one should "present a conclusion" (a judgment, decision, opinion, etc.) that needs a defense; and the following nine should "defend the conclusion with relevant, detailed evidenc"—drawn primarily from general knowledge about the subject.

Note: Underline the thesis as is done in the sample papers. Also, fill out a structure analysis sheet (see sample below) for your themes as has been done for the sample papers. Students can type their own for each paper, or teachers can provide copies of the sample below.

Theme # _____ Name_____ Date_____

Subordination: **Parallelism:**

A. Main Part only   E. Intro., Inter. and MP   A. No parallelism

B. Introduction and MP   F. Intro., Extension and MP   B. Compound

C. Interruption and MP   G. Inter., Extension and MP   C. Series

D. Extension and MP   H. Intro., Inter., Ext.,   D. Compound and
                            and MP   Series

1____1____   6____6____   11____11____   16____16____   21____21____

2____2____   7____7____   12____12____   17____17____   22____22____

3____3____   8____8____   13____13____   18____18____   23____23____

4____4____   9____9____   14____14____   19____19____   24____24____

5____5____   10____10____   15____15____   20____20____   25____25____

Examples and Commentary

Such an assignment is typical of those students face. Some texts call them body paragraphs. The sentence containing the judgment is referred to as the topic sentence. Even though assignments might vary somewhat from the one above, students can improve their writing by applying what can be learned from Insight #4 about content above.

UNACCEPTABLE EXAMPLE

```
Jon Doe, 4-1

Eng. 121


                             Movies

   (1)Movies are very popular in the U.S.   (2) I don't know what
I would do if I couldn't go to a movie at least once a week.   (3)
Movie stars make a lot of money.   (3) You'd think tey were more
important than the President. (4) I think movies are important and
people shouldn't make fun of them and think their just entertain-
ment.  (5) I mean a person can learn a lot from movies, like about
life and stuff.  (6) I wanted to be a movie star once, when I was
younger.  (7) Most young people are to impressed by movies.  (8)
And they want to be like movie stars. (9) Especially the money they
make and the glamorous life they lead.
```

Theme # _____ Name_____ Date_____

Subordination:

A. Main Part only   E. Intro., Inter. and MP   A. No parallelism

B. Introduction and MP   F. Intro., Extension and MP   B. Compound

C. Interruption and MP   G. Inter., Extension and MP   C. Series

D. Extension and MP   H. Intro., Inter., Ext.,   D. Compound and
                              and MP   Series

Parallelism:

1 _A_ 1 _A_	6 _D_ 6 _B_	11____11____	16____16____	21____21____
2 _A_ 2 _A_	7 _D_ 7 _A_	12____12____	17____17____	22____22____
3 _A_ 3 _A_	8 _A_ 8 _A_	13____13____	18____18____	23____23____
4 _A_ 4 _A_	9 _A_ 9 _A_	14____14____	19____19____	24____24____
5 _A_ 5 _B_	10 _A_ 10 _B_	15____15____	20____20____	25____25____

The first sentence does make a judgment—"are very popular"—but the writer does not proceed to defend it. Consequently, the paper lacks unity and coherence. It jumps around. It is, at best, a collection of random thoughts about movies. The defense sentences lack "relevant, detailed evidence." The student obviously put down anything that came to mind about movies —without any attempt to meet the requirement of the assignment.

Jon Doe, 4-1

Eng. 121

Some movies – unforgettable

(1) <u>Some movies are so famous their titles have become household words</u>. (2) *Titanic* certainly is one of them. (3) It starred Leonardo DiCaprio and Kate Winslet, two extremely popular stars, and has been seen by countless millions all over the world in theaters and on TV. (4) Some children's movies, too, will apparently never be forgotten. (5) Among them, *Cars* and its sequels, all Pixar productions, are very popular. (6) Also—harking to an older era—*The Wizard of Oz*, which starred the very famous Judy Garland, is perhaps the best remembered. (7) Popular for years in theaters across the country, it has also been shown repeatedly on TV networks. (8) Then, too, several older releases have been so extremely popular that practically everyone is aware of them. (9) Their titles—*Slumdog Millionaire*, *Argo*, and the *Harry Potter* films—are referred to over and over again—on TV and radio, on blogs, in newspapers and in conversations. (10) The *Potter* films, some predict, will perhaps set all-time records for revenue: box office, rental and on-demand combined.

Theme # _____ Name_____ Date_____

Subordination:

A. Main Part only   E. Intro., Inter. and MP

B. Introduction and MP   F. Intro., Extension and MP

C. Interruption and MP   G. Inter., Extension and MP

D. Extension and MP   H. Intro., Inter., Ext., and MP

Parallelism:

A. No parallelism

B. Compound

C. Series

D. Compound and Series

1 _A_ 1 _A_	6 _E_ 6 _A_	11___11___	16___16___	21___21___
2 _A_ 2 _A_	7 _B_ 7 _A_	12___12___	17___17___	22___22___
3 _C_ 3 _B_	8 _C_ 8 _A_	13___13___	18___18___	23___23___
4 _C_ 4 _A_	9 _G_ 9 _D_	14___14___	19___19___	24___24___
5 _E_ 5 _A_	10 _G_ 10 _C_	15___15___	20___20___	25___25___

While this paper is perhaps not a brilliant piece of writing, it does begin with a judgment—"are so famous their titles have become household words"—and follows with nine sentences that make a decent defense. Also, the defense is filled with "relevant, detailed evidence." The details include names (Kate Winslet, Leonardo DiCaprio, Judy Garland), titles (*Titanic, Cars, Argo*), media outlets (TV, radio, blogs, newspapers), titles (of many movies.)

As we will note later, the mechanics of the piece (the sentence structure, sentence sense, punctuation, etc.), while not perfect, are certainly acceptable.

Important notice: To write every sentence acceptably in their themes, students must be conscious of the structure of every sentence they write—just as professional writers are.

Note that most sentences in the unacceptable themes are simple AA sentences with very little subordination or parallelism. The acceptable themes, on the other hand, have more detail in many of their sentences—in introductions, interruptions and extensions, and in parallel elements.

Jon Doe, 4-1

Eng. 121

College is important

(1) <u>Going to college is important</u>. (2) So many careers require a college dgree its almost impossible to find a job, unless you have a college degree. (3) The cost of going to college these days is outrages. (4) One of my friends is attending a private college that costs over $30,000. (5) Who can pay that much just to go to college. (6) One thing about going to college though, they can't take it away from you. (7) When a person begins college they should have a definite goal in mind—like a doctor, dentist, lawyer or some preffesion. (8) Doctors, at least those that specilise make a lot of money. (9) Lawyers, especially criminal trial lawyers make a lot of money to. (10) When they become famous like Alan Dershowitz.

Theme # _____ Name_____ Date_____

Subordination:

A. Main Part only

B. Introduction and MP

C. Interruption and MP

D. Extension and MP

E. Intro., Inter. and MP

F. Intro., Extension and MP

G. Inter., Extension and MP

H. Intro., Inter., Ext., and MP

Parallelism:

A. No parallelism

B. Compound

C. Series

D. Compound and Series

1____1____   6____6____   11____11____   16____16____   21____21____

2____2____   7____7____   12____12____   17____17____   22____22____

3____3____   8____8____   13____13____   18____18____   23____23____

4____4____   9____9____   14____14____   19____19____   24____24____

5____5____   10____10____   15____15____   20____20____   25____25____

Jane Doe, 4-1

Eng. 121

U.S. has two basic types of post high school educational institutions

(1) There are, basically, two groups of post-high school educational institutions in the U.S. (2) In one group, there are the typical undergraduate/graduate schools—usually called colleges or universities. (3) They offer the typical liberal arts and pre-professional courses that lead to four-year degrees and entrance to graduate schools. (4) In most instances, these schools are four-year colleges—private and public—and large universities. (5) But, some in this group—and the number has increased over the years—are two-year community colleges that provide courses for the first two years of a four-year degree program. (6) The other basic group of post high school institutions is comprised, for the most part, of vocational or technical schools. (7) These generally offer one- and two-year programs in vocational areas—such as auto mechanics, computer science, nursing and the like—that do not require a four-year degree. (8) Unlike undergraduate programs, vocational-technical courses deal, almost exclusively, with one special trade area: one exclusively with carpentry, another just with welding, another only with computer programming. (9) General education courses—such as English, history, art—are not generally required in vocational-technical curriculums—as they are in undergraduate programs. (10) Basically, the U.S. has these two types of post high school education available: undergraduate/graduate schools and vocational-technical schools.

UNACCEPTABLE EXAMPLE (COMMENTARY):

Again, the topic sentence does make a judgment—"is important." But, saying something is important is so vague and general a reader cannot predict what the nature of the defense will be, and such theses for a piece of writing are seldom considered acceptable.

Again, too, the defense is deplorable. It gets off the point by drifting into costs, goals and income of doctors and lawyers—a completely unacceptable defense and development.

ACCEPTABLE EXAMPLE (COMMENTARY):

This paper could, of course, be improved; but, in view of the assignment—a defense "drawn primarily from general knowledge"—it is certainly acceptable. The judgment—that "there are two groups of post high school educational institutions in the U.S."—is perhaps dangerously close to being too obvious; but it is not unlike generalizations often made by professional writers to warrant an explanation of some aspect of their subject. The defense, too, is perhaps somewhat general; but there are specifics also—"community colleges," "auto mechanics, computer science, nursing," "carpentry . . . welding . . . computer programming," "English, history, art."

Note that this short paper ends with a summary—or clincher sentence—that repeats the thesis—the judgment presented and defended in the theme. Use of such a summary statement is generally an option for the writer. If an assignment indicates that such a clincher statement be used, however, a student should, of course, be careful to do so.

Writing Assignment 4-2

Sample Theses

Create three possible theses a writer could present and defend about any of these sample subject areas: education, sports, politics or entertainment.

Note: Since you do not have to defend these theses, they can be judgments that would be very difficult to defend in a paper.

Example: Some movies have been very expensive to produce.

A good defense of the above thesis would likely require some research in magazines, newspapers or online entertainment sites to find out how much money was spent on some specific movies.

ACCEPTABLE EXAMPLES

1) The federal No Child Left Behind teaching standards have been criticized by some education organizations. (The defense could name the organizations and summarize some of their criticisms)

2) The new Major League Baseball rules are not very popular with some managers. (The defense could identify the managers and quote their expressions of discontent)

3) Some recent movies deal with several very controversial social issues. (The defense could name the titles of the movies and identify the social issues each deals with)

UNACCEPTABLE EXAMPLES

1) The U.S. has a good school system. (The judgment is too broad and general; the type of defense cannot be anticipated)

2) Are digital media tools contributing to social problems among teenagers? (This does not make a judgment)

3) Joe Mauer, the first baseman for the Minnesota Twins, makes $23 million per season. (This is a factual statement that doesn't require any defense; such statements are often used as part of the defense of some judgment)

WRITING ASSIGNMENT 4-3: BRIEF DESCRIPTION

Write a one-paragraph **description** of some object or scene that you have **observed**. The defense and development should be made primarily with **examples** and **details**. The organization should basically consist of simple **enumeration** (listing) of examples and detail.

Note: Find a spot on campus—in the cafeteria or the commons, for instance—or some other public place and spend some time taking notes from the scene. Record what you see, smell, hear, observe.

Procedure: Make a conclusion (judgment) about some object or scene that you have observed. Express that conclusion in the first sentence (topic sentence). Complete the paragraph with an enumeration of examples and details that directly and adequately defend the judgment.

Note: If the source of your detailed information is observation, be accurate; if it is imagination, be plausible.

Content: In the first example, the writer expresses a judgment—specifically in the phrase "appeared to be expensively furnished." The examples and details in the other sentence make that judgment (conclusion) seem reasonable. Specific

---

```
ACCEPTABLE EXAMPLE

Jon Doe, 4-3
Eng. 121

        Furnishings appear
         to be expensive


   The home office certainly appeared
to be expensively furnished. The
carpet was luxurious—a hand-woven
piece covering maple floorboards. A
desk and table, both made of sol-
id cherry, sat in one corner. The
chairs and loveseat were modern
Scandinavian: natural-wood colored,
straight-lined, lightly upholstered.
On the wall hung framed works of ab-
stract art. Floor-to-ceiling book-
cases lined two walls; both of them
were filled with books, photographs
and sculptures. A flat screen TV and
stereo components—a five-disc CD play-
er, DVD player and Bose speakers—sat
on a long walnut console. And thick
white blinds covered windows that
overlooked a brick patio. Obviously,
much money had been spent in furnish-
ing and decorating the room.
```

---

details—such as "solid cherry," "framed works," "Bose speakers," etc.—make the first example much better than the second. Specificity is extremely important in all types of writing.

The second example, on the following page, presents a judgment well enough, but the defense and development is too general and irrelevant. Where the detailed defense should be, new judgments are presented: "Some people say...," "Everyone has a right...," etc. These generalizations are not closely enough related to the main idea to be used in the paragraph.

Organization: The structure in the first theme is about as simple as it can be and is often used in paragraph organization. An outline would be a mere listing of the defense as follows:

Main idea (topic sentence): The home office certainly appeared to be expensively furnished.

I. Hand-woven carpet
II. Cherry desk and table
III. Scandinavian chairs and loveseat
IV. Framed abstract art
V. Floor-to-ceiling bookcases
VI. TV and stereo components
VII. Thick white blinds

Coherence in the first theme is no problem because all the examples and details directly relate to and defend the idea (judgment) in the first sentence.

Shaded areas=defense:

Since a piece of writing is made up of conclusion and defense of conclusions, and since the student of writing must learn to distinguish one from the other, the sentences in these sample papers that basically present conclusions are left unshaded while the sentences that basically present defense are shaded.

Note: In the research paper, the conclusions—the thesis, division ideas, topic sentences and primary ideas plus introductory, transitional and concluding elements—are not shaded and are not documented with parenthetical citations or footnotes. The defense material, on the other hand, is. The secondary and tertiary statements—sentences filled with specific detail from source material—that directly defend major conclusions are shaded and generally are documented.

UNACCEPTABLE EXAMPLE

Jane Doe, 4-3
Eng. 121

Luxury!

The home office certainly appeared to be expensively furnished. The room was filled with expensive furniture. Like the nice flat screen TV. A DVD player and Bose speakers, too. You can't buy all those things unless you have a lot of money. Some people would saythe furnishings were modest. Well, that's there business. Everyone has a right to there own oppinon. But I think I can tell weather something was expensive or not and it certainly was.

ACCEPTABLE EXAMPLE

Jon Doe, 4-3
Eng. 121

Cove Point Lodge ideal for couple's retreat

Cove Point Lodge on Lake Superior's North Shore is ideal for couples on a weekend retreat. The cozy rooms, with their fireplaces and broad views of the lake, are perfect for lazy afternoons of reading or watching movies. The high-ceilinged common room—with its stone fireplace, comfy couches and coffee bar—is also a great place to relax. Couples looking for more activity can hike trails, walk along the water or fish for walleye. The nearby Gooseberry Falls offers more trails and beautiful waterfall vistas. During the evening, the lodge restaurant offers intimate, candle-lit dining and an array of wonderful food: fresh walleye, steak and shrimp, Italian entrees and more. For a nightcap, choose from an array of wines or craft beers in the bar area. What could be more ideal for a couple looking to get away for a weekend? Cove Point Lodge is an excellent retreat.

```
┌─────────────────────────────────────────────────────────────────────┐
│  UNACCEPTABLE EXAMPLE                                                │
│                                                                      │
│  Jane  Doe, 4-3                                                      │
│  Eng. 121                                                            │
│                                                                      │
│                        Cove Point Lodge!                            │
│                                                                      │
│      Cove Point Lodge on Lake Superior's North Shore is ideal for   │
│  couples on a weekend retreat.  You should see the rooms!  Some re-  │
│  sorts don't have very good rooms but the rooms at Cove Point Lodge  │
│  are cozy, with fireplaces and movies.  But there is more than that to│
│  do.  Couples can hike trails, walk along the water and fishing for  │
│  walleye.  Then their is nearby Gooseberry Falls.  But doesn't every │
│  resort need a good restaurant?  I was at one once that had bad food.│
│  That's not the way it is at Cove Point Lode.  A great place.        │
│                                                                      │
└─────────────────────────────────────────────────────────────────────┘
```

WRITING INSIGHTS: Discovering the Keys to Structure and Content

Writing Assignment 4-4

Brief Exposition

Write a one-paragraph **explanation** (exposition) of some aspect of a subject about which you have some **general knowledge** as a result of wide reading or experience. The defense and development should be made with any type (or combination of types) that seems appropriate: **example**, **detail**, **definition**, **good analogy**, **logical argument**, **anecdotes**, etc. The organization, however, should be of one type only—comparison (either contrast or similar).

Note: Please note carefully any changes your instructor makes in this assignment.

Procedure: In the first sentence (topic sentence) present a conclusion (judgment) that essentially says two things are alike (similar) or are not alike (contrast). These conclusions (judgments) are generally expressed through synonyms for alike—such as **similar**, **parallels**, **same**, **resembles**, **analogous**, etc. (check a thesaurus for others)—and also through synonyms for not alike—such as **contrast**, **different**, **opposite**, **antithesis**, **dissimilar**, **unlike**, **contrary**, etc. Different forms of these synonyms may also be used, of course. Complete the paragraph with pertinent defense and development—arranged either in two divisions that make a comparison or in some other order that makes an appropriate comparison.

ACCEPTABLE EXAMPLE

Jon Doe, 4-4
Eng. 121

Top leaders come to power differently in democracies, totalitarian governments

Top leaders in a democracy come to power in a different way from those in a totalitarian state. In a democracy leaders are elected. In the U.S. and France, for instance, the top leaders—the Presidents—are elected in open nationwide elections. In countries like England, Canada, Norway and Sweden, the Premiers and Prime Ministers are picked by representatives of the people who have been elected in free nationwide referendums. In totalitarian governments, on the other hand, top leaders come to power in some other way than through elections. They often seize power in a military coup—such as they did recently in Thailand. Often they come to power following a revolution—such as Castro famously did in Cuba. Sometimes, too, the top leader in a totalitarian government is picked by a small minority party that has enough power to control the government—such as the Communist Party in China. The way the top leader comes to power is significantly different in a democracy from what it is under a totalitarian regime.

Content: Both examples say in the first sentence (topic sentence) that two things are not alike. They express this judgment through the synonyms **different** (in the first example) and **opposite** (in the second). In the first theme, the judgment is defended with general knowledge that the writer has about how leaders come to power. In the second theme, the judgment is defended with general knowledge that the writer has about socialism and capitalism.

Note: When using general knowledge as defense and development, be sure that the examples, details, etc. are true and accurate. The information must be generally accepted as true and accurate by fairly well-educated people. Assertions by a small minority group may not be acceptable. Contentions by one authority—if most authorities disagree—generally would not be acceptable.

Organization: Generally, paragraphs using comparison have a simple two-division organization—a division for each of the two things being compared. Other types of order may be used, however. One popular approach is to show both sides of a point before moving on to the next.

Notice the use of the transitional expression "on the other hand" to show contrast and to move smoothly to the second division.

ACCEPTABLE EXAMPLE

Jane Doe, 4-4
Eng. 121

Socialism and capitalism —economic opposites

Socialism and capitalism are completely opposite economic orders. Socialism is basically government control of the economic forces within a nation. In countries considered socialistic, for instance, the government owns and manages the manufacturing plants, the mines, the oil wells. In these countries the government also owns and controls the organizations used to distribute goods and services—for instance, the railroads, the stores, the warehouses. In countries considered capitalistic, on the other hand, private individuals and companies own and control the facilities that produce and distribute goods and services. Almost all production—such as farming, manufacturing and mining—is carried out by private corporations. Distribution of goods—except for that which is carried on by the country's postal services—is primarily done by private industry—railroads, trucking firms, shipping lines, airlines. The basic structure of socialism is just the opposite of the basic structure of capitalism.

Mechanics and Format: Notice how the expression "such as" is used. Students often use this expression incorrectly by placing it in the main sentence rather than in the interruption or extension where it generally should be. Remember, the colon or the dash should generally come before—not after—"such as."

Writing Assignment 4-5

Brief Analysis

Write a one-paragraph **content analysis** of some aspect of **an article or story** you have read and studied and can, as you write, refer to specifically. You must have the article in your possession as you write, in other words. Use information from the article or story—**examples**, **details**, **quotes** (direct and indirect), **names**, **dates**, etc.—for defense and development. For organization use **logical division** or **logical order**.

Procedure: Make a judgment (a conclusion) relevant to some subject alluded to in the article or story. Present the judgment in the first sentence (topic sentence). Complete the paragraph with pertinent defense material—drawn primarily from the article or story analyzed.

Content: Both examples of assignment 4-5 begin with judgments that are logical in view of the details contained within the articles analyzed and in view of the details taken from the articles themselves to defend and develop those judgments.

ACCEPTABLE EXAMPLE

Jon Doe, 4-5
Eng. 121

Parker argues against 'trigger warnings' in literature

In a recent column, "Fair warning, provoking a thought is literature's job," Kathleen Parker objects to demands for "trigger warnings"—labels on works of literature designed to protect college students from content that might offend or bother them. Parker, a *Washington Post* columnist, argues that college is precisely the place where people should be exposed to controversial ideas. "Without making light of anyone's ethnicity, race or trauma, especially rape or stress disorder suffered by veterans," she writes, "such precautions are misplaced in an institution of higher learning where one is expected to be intellectually challenged and where one's psychological challenges are expected to be managed elsewhere." Moreover, Parker notes that literary criticism also demands that readers understand the times in which a work was written. "Thus," she writes, "when the egregiously offensive N-word appears in The Adventures of Huckleberry Finn, is it too much to ask that readers reflect upon the word's usage when Mark Twain wrote the book?"

INSIGHT #4: Thesis

```
ACCEPTABLE EXAMPLE

Jane Doe, 4-5
Eng. 121

              Zakaria calls for moderate
              Voices in the Arab World

     Fareed Zakaria, in a recent *Time* column, wonders whether moder-
ates in the Arab world will stand up to religious extremism.  In "A
Moment for Moderates," he answers his own question with "a cautious
and tentative yes."  Zakaria notes that Wael Ghonim—a leading democracy
activist in Egypt—used Facebook to denounce violent mobs of extremists
who were calling for the death of a filmmaker who made a controversial
video about the Prophet Muhammad.  While admitting that he has often de-
scribed Muslim moderates as "cowardly and defensive," Zakaria now lauds
them for stepping forward.  "In several countries where the protests took
place, many have criticized the extremists and urged people to voice
their opposition to the video in peaceful ways," he writes.  Zakaria
also notes that as Muslim societies are moving toward democracy in the
wake of the Arab Spring, more voices are being heard.  "Many are nasty,
intolerant and bigoted," he writes.  "But others, like those of Libyans
Mohamed el-Magariaf and Mahmoud Jibril, are moderate and modern."
```

NOTES:

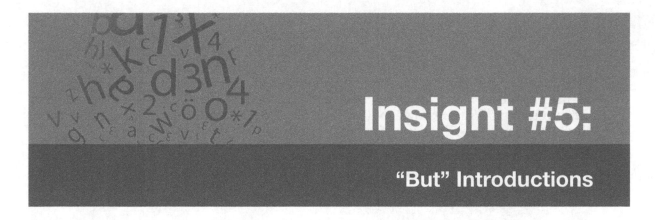

Insight #5:

"But" Introductions

Most pieces of writing do not begin with the thesis (the opinion, the judgment, the conclusion) or the defense of that thesis. Rather, they begin with material that draws the reader toward that thesis and eventual defense. That leads us to another important <u>insight</u> that students of writing must acquire insofar as <u>content</u> is concerned: an awareness of <u>how theses are presented</u>.

INSIGHT #5:   ***Content***: Writers generally begin with an appropriate introduction to the thesis—often with a "but" introduction or some subtle variation of it that alludes to the opposite view (judgment, position, etc.) of the thesis.

    As noted earlier, writers do not generally begin their pieces with the thesis. How, then, do they begin? That is the question frequently, and reasonably, asked by students of composition. How do I start? Insight #5 answers that important question.

    Note the following "but" introductions used by professional writers:

Star Tribune, May 16, 2014	**USA Today, May 20, 2014**	**Washington Post, May 30, 2014**
Barack Obama's presidency was supposed to restore America's good name in the world... <u>But early this month, the ... *Economist* published a cover story reminding us that the world is Goldilocks fussy when it comes to the way America wields its (super) power.</u>	On May 17, we will celebrate the 60th anniversary of ... *Brown v. Board of Education*. ... ...this...will...prompt many solemn pronouncements that... our schools are just as segregated as ever ... <u>But this is not true.</u>	WARSAW – By any measure, it was a landmark, landslide victory — for Europe. ... <u>Yet in his victory speech, (Petro) Poroshenko declared he wanted not only to "put an end to war...," but also to "bring in European values"</u> ...

In each example above, the first sentences—or "leads," as journalists call them—allude to the judgments about the subject or issue that everyone normally accepts—almost stereotype positions. But these judgments are not right, correct, true, according to the writer. So essentially the writer says, "This is the way people think it is" (introduction), but "this is the way it really is" (thesis). (Note the use of the word "yet"—a synonym for "but" or "however"—in the third example.)

Students must learn to consciously write "but" introductions. They are one of the "tricks of the trade" professional writers know about and exploit. Students need the advantage of knowing about this rather simple device that professional writers seem to use so extensively.

Writing Assignment 5-1

"But" introductions

Write a four-sentence "but" introduction for one of the following theses:

Note: Good theses very often present a position that is opposite from what people generally accept about the subject or issue. Introductions to theses often remind readers of judgments made about the issue, and, then, continue with "But" and the thesis. To emphasize this point, the following theses drastically contrast with generally accepted positions. Luckily, students don't have to defend them in this assignment. They merely have to introduce them; but they should do so, of course, as though they think the thesis is true.

Choose one of the following theses:

1. But, the birthdays of children should not be celebrated as they are currently being done. [used in examples; should not be selected]
2. But, more energy—more gas, oil, coal, etc.—should be used, not less.
3. But, there should be a national effort to reduce consumption of red meat.
4. But, it is good for one's health to be somewhat overweight.
5. But, a college degree does not always provide the easy access to a good paying job that it once did.

UNACCEPTABLE EXAMPLES

Jon Doe, 5-1
Eng. 121

Extravagant birthdays

(1) Have you ever thought about the birthdays of children? (2) Well, I have—especially about how their celebrated! (3) Children expect to much from birthdays. (4) They are more interested in the gifts than in the people who come to there parties. (5) But the birthdays of children should not be celebrated as extravagantly as they often are these days.

OR

Jane Doe, 5-1
Eng. 121

Birthday Parties--too much

(1) Children look forward to there birthdays. (2) They usually recieve gifts at a party, to which there friends and relatives have been invited. (3) That's the way birthday parties should be. (4) But parties today involve going to Nickelodeon Universe at the Mall of America or similar places, and the cost becomes prohibitive. (5) But birthdays of children should not be celebrated as extravagantly as they often are these days.

6. But, the sale of big cars is holding up quite well.
7. But, the price of gasoline should be much higher than it is now.

Note: In writing the four sentences that lead into the thesis, be careful to follow these guidelines:
1. Avoid defending the thesis in any way. That is a no-no! All defense must follow the presentation of the thesis.
2. Pack a lot of detail into the four sentences—examples, explanations, etc.—by using some introductions, interruptions and extensions.
3. Make sure the four sentences read well with the thesis. Rewrite them until they do.
4. Create a title that reflects [is an abbreviation of] the thesis:

The first example above does not present "the opposite view of the thesis." It begins with some weak, trite expressions about the subject (sentences 1 and 2) and follows those with sentences that defend the thesis—a no-no. The title merely identifies the subject; it does not reflect the judgment of the thesis. The word "extravagant" does have a negative connotation; but it is too weak to reflect the strong judgment of the thesis—"should not be celebrated as extravagantly as they are."

The second example begins appropriately enough-with an explanation of what is generally accepted about the subject and the issue, which is also "the opposite view of the thesis." But then it slips into a defense sentence (4). The title—while perhaps not brilliant—does come close to reflecting the thesis and is certainly acceptable.

Notice that both examples "do not read well"—the first four sentences "do not read well" with the thesis. In the first example, the first four sentences do not contrast with the thesis enough to warrant the use of the transitional "but." In the second example, sentence (4) does not contrast enough with the thesis.

The first example is a typical "but" lead-in (introduction). It tells the reader about the way things are—about the popular accepted conclusions (decisions, judgments) concerning birthdays. Then, with the transitional word "but," it hits the reader with a thesis (a judgment) that conflicts—that is quite different, as many good theses are.

The second example presents the usual view in a novel way. It briefly describes one birthday, recognizes that it is considered ideal and then says "but" it should not be that way. There are many ways a writer can inform the reader about "how things are" with a subject.

The titles are, again, perhaps not brilliant, but they do reflect (are abbreviations of) the thesis and therefore are acceptable. A title such as "Kids Dream Party Can Become a Parent's Nightmare" doesn't quite reflect the thesis, but it might be used if the defense is about parent's problems with big elaborate parties.

The use of introductions, interruptions and extensions in these acceptable examples was obviously done consciously. If the student had not been aware of them, errors in punctuation and usage would undoubtedly have been made. Deliberate and conscious use of subordination improves the mechanics of any piece of writing.

ACCEPTABLE EXAMPLES

Jon Doe, 5-1
Eng. 121

Some birthday parties are too extravagant

(1) Birthday parties are big events in the lives of children. (2) Their friends and relatives bring gifts; their parents provide ice cream and cake and a place to play games. (3) And, it is not unusual for parents to make the event a really big affair by taking everyone to Chuck E. Cheese's, a movie, an amusement park or some such special place. (4) Then, too, expensive gifts are not unusual: bicycles, iPads, video games, smart phones, sometimes even horses or expensive trips. (5) <u>But, the birthdays of children should not be celebrated as extravagantly as they often are these days.</u>

OR

Jane Doe, 5-1
Eng. 121

Birthday parties should not be such a big deal

(1) It was James Dickey's seventh birthday. (2) To celebrate the event, his parents bought him a new bicycle, took him and his friends—sixteen boys and girls about his age—to Chuck E. Cheese's for pizza and games and then to an amusement park for rides unlimited. (3) It was an ideal evening for the seventeen youngsters. (4) It was the kind of birthday party every kid dreams about. (5) <u>But, birthdays of children should not be celebrated as extravagantly as they often are these days.</u>

<u>Theses vary</u> a great deal. Some are highly controversial—such as those used in editorials, political columns, analyses stories, etc. Some are safe conclusions—almost considered factual because they are so widely accepted as being true. News stories, sports stories, columns, etc. often use subjective, debatable theses and defend them as best they can.

<u>Conclusion making</u>—as the writer must do to create a thesis—is a very human activity. People very often say, "I think that . . ." The product of thinking is a conclusion—usually a conclusion (decision, judgment, opinion) about what is—or is not—true. Much of humankind's activity is used to try to discover truth. All people—in conversations—present and defend what they think is true—their conclusions (judgments, opinions) what they think is true, proper, just, etc. Writers put it in writing.

<u>Since conclusion making</u> is such a prevalent human activity, we have many synonyms for the product: conclusions, judgments, opinions, positions, etc. Below are listed those which are most widely used:

appraisals	**deductions**	**opinions**	**statements**
assertions	**evaluations**	**philosophy**	**suppositions**
assumptions	**feelings**	**points**	**theorems**
attitudes	**judgments**	**positions**	**theories**
beliefs	**inferences**	**premises**	**theses**
comments	**generalizations**	**pronouncements**	**viewpoints**
contentions	**hypotheses**	**postulates**	**views**
decisions	**ideas**	**solutions**	**. . .others**

Some scholars might insist that there is a difference in the meaning of these words; but writers seem to use them—whichever synonym seems suitable—to identify their own, or someone else's conclusion (judgment, opinion, position). It is true that writers tend to use the fancier, learned synonyms to identify those conclusions that are arrived at after careful study. (They do not refer to "Darwin's opinion," for instance; they use <u>theory</u>.) And writers tend to use the more common synonyms—opinion, judgment, etc.—for conclusions that are arrived at very quickly without much study. But the terms are often used almost interchangeably—without much thought as to how the conclusion was created.

Writers try to use detailed facts (truths)—names, dates, titles, places, quotes, etc.—to defend their theses. Below are listed some of the words we use generally to identify, more specifically, what kind of "relevant, detailed evidence" a writer uses:

anecdotes	**names**
definitions	**personal experiences**
details	**places**
dates	**objective reports**
examples	**scientific data**
expert opinions	**statistics**
explanations	**titles**
general knowledge	**quotes**
historical records	**. . .others**

Insight #6:

Detail in Writing

Much of the material that writers use in their work consists of details and other information that serve to defend the thesis and to add context and interest to the writing. To this end, another important <u>insight</u> that students of writing must acquire—insofar as <u>content</u> is concerned—is an awareness of <u>how details are used</u> in writing.

INSIGHT #6: ***Content***: Writers glean detail—from their reading, from hobbies, from school courses, from work experiences, from research, etc.— to include in the defense of their theses.

Professional writers obviously take notes on details about the subjects they intend to write about. They record names, dates, places, times, titles, statistics, quotes, etc. that they can use, in addition to general knowledge, to create the defense in their pieces of writing.

In most writing, the defense is a combination of details from general knowledge, reading and research. In a research paper, of course, the details that can come from only one or a few sources need to be footnoted or acknowledged in parenthetical citations. But in most writing details that appear in most news magazines and newspapers are not footnoted nor are the sources even alluded to. If the material comes basically form one source, writers often make an allusion to it with expressions such as "A recent article in *Time* indicated that . . ." "The Encyclopedia Americana notes that . . ." "It is, according to recent studies reported in The New York Times, a non-union . . ." A few token references to sources are often made by newspaper reporters but should be used sparingly in student papers. Examples: "Experts say . . ." "Reliable sources noted . . ." "Some observers said . . ."

Name _____ Date _____

Writing Assignment 6-1

15-sentence theme

Write a 15-sentence theme. Use four sentences of lead-in to introduce the thesis, one sentence to present the thesis, nine sentences to defend the thesis and one sentence to recast the thesis (the concluding sentence).

Note: Be careful to use detail in the defense. In addition to general knowledge about the subject, get some detail from newspaper, magazine or online stories on the subject; find some names, dates, titles or statistics, etc. in those stories that can be used in your writing. Similar details for some subjects can, of course, be found in texts, encyclopedias, etc. These details are used in these sources for a purpose, but you will use them for a new purpose—to defend your thesis. And, since such details are for the most part general knowledge, you do not have to credit the source, in most instances.

The paper to the right is acceptable because it begins with an appropriate introduction to the thesis (Insight #5), because it clearly "presents the thesis and defends it with relevant, detailed evidence" (Insight #4) and because it uses details "gleaned from reading" (research) —possibly from current newspaper and magazine articles on the subject (Insight #6).

ACCEPTABLE EXAMPLE

Jon Doe, 6-1
Eng. 121

College Football—More than Notre Dame and USC

On any given Saturday in the fall, as many as two dozen college football games are broadcast on television. These contests, between teams from some of the largest and best-known colleges and universities in the country, are immensely popular and draw a wide viewership. Elite athletes from across the nation compete in these games, offering fans thrilling entertainment. Some of these players, no doubt, will go on to play professional football.

However, there are also many small-college teams that compete in lower divisions each weekend.

Several teams play at the NCAA Division II and III levels. For instance, in the state of Minnesota alone, more than 20 schools field teams that compete in Division II or III conferences. One of those schools, The University of Minnesota-Duluth, won Division II national championships in both 2008 and 2010. Another, St. John's University, won Division III national titles in 1976 and 2003. Not

---

Note: In longer, more formal research papers, students would generally have to footnote (document) the sources of these details—the dates, names, titles, quotes, etc.

While the paper is not perfect mechanically, it certainly is acceptable in view of the assignment. The writer shows a great deal of "sentence sense." She uses subordination and parallelism very well and follows most of the conventions (the practices, rules) of good writing.

Note: The minor mistakes—noted with abbreviations and numbers—might lower a grade somewhat (depending on various requirements made for specific assignments), but for most writing assignments, papers written in this manner would generally receive a good grade.

```
counting the playoffs, Division II
teams play 11 games while Division III
teams play 10 games each season.
     Moreover, several other schools
have teams that compete at the com-
munity college level. Minnesota, in
fact, has 11 community college teams
that play in the NJCAA—about half of
them in northern Minnesota and the
other half in the southern part of
the state. The teams are split into
two divisions, with the top four teams
from each division competing in a con-
ference tournament. In 2011, Roches-
ter Community and Technical College
played in the Graphic Edge Bowl—one
of nine bowl games sponsored by the
NJCAA.
     So even though major college foot-
ball dominates the television land-
scape, many other teams compete at the
small-college level each weekend.
```

WHAT ABOUT PARAGRAPHS?

Note: Specific directions for indenting to indicate new paragraphs are not easy to prescribe, especially in view of current practices. In most newspapers and magazines, every sentence or two is indented—primarily to provide "white space."

Paragraphing as is done in the first example above is not unusual, because each contains an important element. The first paragraph contains the introduction to the thesis, the second states the thesis and the third and fourth each present an area of defense. Paragraphing in the second paper is not so logical, but is consistent with what is done in much of professional writing. The thesis is included in the first paragraph, along with the introduction to the thesis. The second and third paragraphs each deal with an area of defense, as was done in the first paper.

But, since there is a clincher statement in the second paper, which the first one does not have, that was, sensibly, put in a separate paragraph.

Professional writers, it seems, do not often use the classic types of paragraphs often studied in many composition courses—introductory, transitional, clincher (or concluding) and body paragraphs. But they do present these same elements. They might, for instance, use three short two or three sentence paragraphs to present what a classic introductory paragraph would contain. And they might use a string of short paragraphs to construct what is generally contained in the classic body paragraph. Consequently, a study of these classic paragraphs can be helpful, and if an assignment calls for their use, a student should, of course, be careful to do so.

Writers basically start a new paragraph whenever they move to a new major element—whenever they move, for instance, from a statement of the thesis to an area of defense, from one area of defense to another, from an area of defense to a digression of some sort to explain, define, concede, analyze, etc., from an area of defense to a transition, summary, call for action, comparison, etc. that a writer often needs to include.

In professional writing, paragraphing—it seems, then—is done as sensibly as possible to meet the needs of the structure and the elements used and follows as closely as possible the conventions that have evolved through publishers' stylebooks and composition texts.

Themes like the unacceptable one to the right are usually dashed off minutes before the assignment is due. Much of the defense includes trite generalizations, easily and quickly made, that also need defending and make for poor evidence. Good writing takes time—to find details for defense, to check spellings of words not frequently used, to organize adequate areas of defense, to plan an introduction that reads well, etc.

Note how almost every sentence has a simple main part-only structure, with very little parallelism. Whenever possible, student writers need to deliberately add introductions, interruptions and extensions—and compounds and series—to their sentences to assure adequate detail.

UNACCEPTABLE EXAMPLE

Jane Doe, 6-1
Eng. 121

College Football

A lot of college football games are on television. Some big-time schools play in these games for our entertainment. Some of these athletes are elite. Some of these players, for sure, will go on to play in the pros.

<u>However, there are also many small-college teams that compete in lower divisions each weekend.</u>

Several teams play in D-II and D-III. Not everybody can play for the big schools. Minnesota has a bunch of schools in those divisions. A few have one championships--The University of Minnesota-Duluth in 2008 and 2010 in D-II and St. John's University won it all in Division III a couple of times, too. Division II teams play 11 games while Division III teams play 10 games each season.

Minnesota has some jucos, too. Minnesota, in fact, has 11 community college teams that play in the NJCAA – about half up north and the other half down south. There are two divisions. In 2011, Rochester Community and Technical College played in the Graphic Edge Bowl—some kind of bowl for small schools.

So even though major college football dominates television, you can still watch a lot of small schools play.

Writing Assignment 6-2

Subject Analysis

OTHER POSSIBLE ASSIGNMENTS

Write a four- or five-paragraph **analysis** of some aspect of some **subject you have researched**, primarily in reference books, textbooks, magazine articles or newspaper stories. Defense and development can be made with any type (or combination of types) that seem appropriate. For such a paper, however, it would generally be made with specific information from articles in reference books, texts, magazines, etc. about your subject—such as **details, examples, quotes, titles, names, statistics,** etc. Organization should be one of the following: **enumeration, logical division, logical order or comparison.**

Procedure: Make a conclusion (judgment) about some aspect of the subject you have carefully studied (researched). Present that judgment (main idea) is a short introductory paragraph. Such a judgment is called the thesis.

Note: Much of what students write— and much of what journalists write—is based on what they have read, studied, researched. Most writing presents a conclusion that seems logical in view of what has been studied. The conclusion is then defended with detailed information from what has been studied.

Writers proceed in many subtle ways to create a conclusion and find appropriate defense and development for it. Per-

---

Jon Doe, 6-2
Eng. 122

Civil Rights Movement inspired generation of leaders

The Civil Rights Movement, one of the most powerful grassroots movements in U.S. history, is often credited with creating a more just and equitable society. The movement led to the passage of two bills—the Civil Rights Act and the Voting Rights Act—that did two important things: banned discrimination in public places and paved the way for African Americans to vote in southern states. <u>But even though the movement reached its peak in the 1960s, it has continued to have a major impact on American society by inspiring a generation of African-Americans to run for public office.</u> It's not a stretch to say that American government would have fewer African-American leaders today had the Civil Rights Movement of the 1950s and 1960s not largely achieved its goals.

One of these leaders, longtime U.S. Rep. John Lewis, was a young protégé of Martin Luther King, Jr., when King was emerging as the Civil Rights Movement's leading spokesman.

---

haps after merely reading widely about some subject, the writer comes to some tentative conclusion he feels he can—with some further study and research—find the information he needs to defend and develop it. If he does find the information, he has everything he needs for a paper. Or, early in his study and research of a subject, he may come to some tentative conclusions, and as he studies may take notes on information that supports that conclusion. If he finds enough information to adequately defend his conclusion, he has what he needs for a paper. The way in which a writer proceeds is perhaps irrelevant and he may need to use different approaches to for different assignments. Basically, however, he must create some conclusions and defend them.

Content: The details are so specific that the writer could have acquired them only through some study and research on these authors. He also had to have ready access to this information. He either had to have note cards on which he had recorded this information, or he had to have the books, articles, etc. in his possession so he could refer to them as he wrote. The details are such that the writer could not have recalled them from his wide reading of the subject. Details of your paper or theme should be equally specific.

Thesis: The Civil Rights Movement inspired many African-Americans to run for public office.

I. John Lewis learned from Martin Luther King, Jr.
   A. Gained experience chairing SNCC
   B. Movement's success led to campaign for office
II. Jesse Jackson got start at 1960s rallies
   A. Emerged as strong voice of black community

For a time, Lewis also served as chairman of the Student Nonviolent Coordinating Committee, a famous organization that took part in sit-ins and freedom rides (Lewis and D'Orso 200). In his book, *Walking With the Wind: A Memoir of the Movement*, Lewis recounts how those heady days contributed to his own decision to run for public office. "Now that the primary purpose of those years of action—securing the right to vote—had been achieved," he writes, "it was time to show black Americans in the South not only that they could select their political representatives but that it was possible to become those representatives" (429). Lewis was eventually elected to the U.S. House of Representatives, from a district in Georgia, and has served in Congress for nearly three decades.

Another well-known African-American leader, Jesse Jackson—twice a candidate for the presidency in the 1980s—honed his skills as an orator at civil rights rallies in the 1960s. Jackson was also an acolyte of King and was with the civil rights leader when he was murdered by a sniper in Memphis, Tenn., on April 4, 1968 (Frady 226-227). The biographer Marshall Frady, in *Jesse: The Life and Pilgrimage of Jesse Jackson*, writes that Jackson's stature as a leader rose along with his relentless activism in the years after King's death. Eventually, Frady writes, "... while most other civil rights activists had peeled off into more personal and parochial orbits, Jackson succeeded in navigating his own way to emerge, at the end of the seventies, as virtually the sole national voice of the black community" (296). While he never won the presidency himself, Jackson has had a long and influential career as the director of the Rainbow Coalition, a civil rights organization based in Chicago, his hometown.

Finally, Barack Obama, who reached the height of public service when he was elected to the presidency in 2008,

III. Barack Obama credited movement as driving force
    A. Studied Civil Rights figures
    B. Movement excited his imagination

Note: In outlines, similar entries—such as for I, II and III—should be kept alike grammatically as much as possible—even though the information will appear in a different form in the paper. In the sample paper, for instance, item I from the outline says Lewis "was a protégé of" Martin Luther King, Jr. The outline entry was changed to "learned from Martin Luther King, Jr." so that it would be more grammatically aligned with items I and II in the outline.

Content: In the second example, the introductory paragraph has the simple three-part organization used in most multi-paragraph papers. The first part—the **preliminary**, **"lead in" information**—extends through the third sentence—through "...a poem or an essay." The next part—the fourth sentence—presents **the thesis**—complete with a synonym for "but"—the word "however." Following the thesis is the third part that presents a preview of the defense and development: two areas that will be developed as defense—American and British literary figures.

Asterisks in themes: If the sample paper on the following page was a division in a documented research paper, the sentences followed by asterisks would be documented. Note also that they are the sentences which defend—with detail—the conclusions in the paragraph and are therefore shaded.

Organization: The organization is a simple one very often used for short multi-paragraph papers. It has two logical divisions. One body paragraph is devoted to each. An outline shows its simplicity:

credited the Civil Rights Movement as a driving force in his life and often talked about civil rights leaders during his campaign. Obama was too young to have taken part in marches or other activities related to the movement; after all, he was only a child when the Civil Rights Act and the Voting Rights Act were passed. However, he read widely about the major figures in the movement—including Lewis and King—when he was a student, according to the biographer David Remnick (13). Remnick, in *The Bridge: The Life and Rise of Barack Obama*, captures the powerful impact the movement had on the future president, writing: "Scenes of the movement's most terrifying and triumphant moments—dogs tearing at marchers, King on the steps of the Lincoln Memorial, his assassination on the balcony of the Lorraine Motel, in Memphis—unspooled in his mind … exciting his imagination and deepening his longing for a firm identification with African-American community and history and for a sense of purpose in his life" (13). Obama used what he learned about the Civil Rights Movement in his work as a community organizer in Chicago and as an instructor at Chicago Law School and, later, in his campaigns for the U.S. Senate and the presidency.

So even though the Civil Rights Movement reached its pinnacle in the 1960s—when it led to the passage of important legislation as well as changes in social attitudes toward African-Americans—its influence is still very evident in American society. Importantly, it has continued to inspire a generation of African-Americans to serve their country through public life, and will certainly inspire more. In that sense, the movement has never really ended.

Thesis: Many famous authors began writing as newspaper reporters.

    I. Famous American authors
       A. Mark Twain
       B. Ernest Hemingway
       C. Sinclair Lewis
       D. John Steinbeck
   II. Famous British authors
       A. Graham Greene
       B. Lawrence Durrell
       C. Aldous Huxley
       D. Winston Churchill

Note: Outlines for longer papers usually indicate the substance of the major conclusions within the paper—the thesis, division topics, topic sentences and primary support ideas. This paper is so short the body paragraphs are the divisions. Consequently, the outline alludes to the thesis, the topic sentences (I and II), and the primary support ideas (A, B, C and D) under each Roman Numeral.

```
            Works Cited

Frady, Marshall.   Jesse: The Life and
     Pilgrimage of Jesse Jackson. New
     York: Random House, 1996.  Print.

Lewis, John, and Michael D'Orso.
     Walking with the Wind: A Memoir
     of the Movement. New York: Simon &
     Schuster, 1998. Print.

Remnick, David.   The Bridge: The Life
     and Rise of Barack Obama.  New
     York: Alfred A. Knopf,    2010.
     Print.
```

```
Jane Doe, 6-1
Eng. 122

            Journalism - good training
              for literary profession

    Among many students, journalism—especially the writing of news sto-
ries—is viewed negatively—something almost beneath a serious student
of composition.  It is not unusual for students to think of reporting
and editing as something very much apart from the world of literature.
Even those students who profess an interest in writing often prefer to
do something more literary than news stories—perhaps a short story, a
play, a poem or an essay.  Many famous authors, however, began writing
as reporters on newspapers.  In fact, some of the most prominent Amer-
ican and British literary figures were, early in their writing careers,
newspapermen, very much involved in the world of journalism.
    Some very renowned U.S. authors began their careers as newspaper
reporters.  Mark Twain was one of them.  After the civil war, he worked
on newspapers in Nevada and California.*  His first successful book, The
Innocents Abroad, was a collection of travel stories he wrote while
working as a reporter for the San Francisco Alto Californian.*  Ernest
Hemingway also began his writing career as a reporter.  After graduating
from high school, he went to work for the Kansas City Star.*  During his
stay in France after World War I, he was a foreign correspondent for the
```

*Toronto Star.** Sinclair Lewis was another famous U.S. author who was a newspaperman before he became a literary figure. After graduating from Yale in 1908, he spent seven years in New York City "reporting, editing and writing advertising," according to one account.* When Lewis decided to become a fulltime freelance writer, he quit his job as advertising manager for the firm of George N. Doran.* John Steinbeck spent some time as a reporter, too. When he left Stanford, he went to New York where he worked for a short time on *The American*, a newspaper now defunct.* His book, *Once there was a War*, is a collection of stories he wrote as a war correspondent for the *New York Herald Tribune* during World War II.*

Some very distinguished British authors, too, worked on newspapers and magazines before they succeeded in publishing works that made them famous literary figures. Graham Greene, for instance, was a newspaperman before his first novel was published. One account of his life notes that "he first earned his living as a journalist, reviewer and film critic, and attracted attention as novelist with *The Man Within* (1929)."* Lawrence Durrell also spent some time as a journalist. One biographical sketch in *Current Biography* notes that he "served in Cairo from 1941 to 1944 as foreign press service officer in the British information office and in Alexandria in 1944-45 as press attaché."* Aldous Huxley, the famous science writer, also worked for several publications. At one time he was a staff Member of *The Athenaeum* and later worked for the *Westminster Gazette.** Then, too, Winston Churchill—who was a great author as well as a great statesman—began writing as a war correspondent in South Africa. He worked for the *London Morning Post*, covering the Boer War in 1899.*

It has not been unusual, then, for writers to start their careers as journalists—working for some newspaper or magazine. Students, therefore, should not look down their noses at newspaper work. Indeed, so many authors have started their writing careers as journalists, it appears that work as a reporter or editor is almost a requirement for anyone who aspires to be a literary figure.

A student of writing might well ask at this point, "Do these insights apply as well—say, for instance—to book reviews or other forms of criticism? The answer, of course, is "Yes!" If these insights reveal something significant about composition, they must, of course, apply to most other types of writing as well. And they do!

Notice how professional writers begin the following book and film reviews:

The Atlantic, May 6, 2008

On the face of it, the story of an expatriate Dutchman obsessed with playing cricket might not seem to have the makings of a quintessentially American novel. <u>But at its heart, Joseph O'Neill's new book, *Netherland*, is about rehabilitating one's life and chasing the American dream, albeit at a time when that dream has lost a bit of its gloss.</u>

RogerEbert.com, Oct. 4, 2013

Alfonso Cuarón's *Gravity*, about astronauts coping with disaster, is a huge and technically dazzling film. ... <u>But the most surprising and impressive thing about "Gravity" isn't its scale, its suspense, or its sense of wonder; it's that ... it is not primarily a film about astronauts, or space, or even a specific catastrophe.</u>

The New York Times, Sept. 4, 2007

<u>Junot Díaz's *Brief Wondrous Life of Oscar Wao* is a wondrous, not-so-brief first novel that is so original it can only be described as Mario Vargas Llosa meets "Star Trek" meets David Foster Wallace meets Kanye West.</u> It is funny, street-smart and keenly observed...

The first two examples have typical "but" lead-in material (using the "But" introduction strategy discussed in Chapter 5) while the third example begins with the thesis.

As is true of all types of writing, writers use a variety of ways to present their theses. The important point is that writers do clearly present a thesis—usually negative or positive—about their subject, which, in these cases, include two books and a film.

OTHER POSSIBLE ASSIGNMENTS

Writing assignment 7-1:
Book review

Write a four-, five- or six-paragraph **content analysis** (critical review) of **one nonfiction book**. Defense and development should be with **any type** of information from the book that seems appropriate: **examples**, **details**, **quotes**, **names**, **titles**, **statistics**, etc. (indicate in the name group what you use the most of throughout the paper). Organization can be of **any type**: **logical division**, **logical order**, **comparison**, **cause-effect**, etc.

Procedure: Study carefully some aspect of the book that you wish to write about. Take notes (do research) on material that you feel will defend the tentative thesis you are considering about the aspect you are interested in.

Ultimately, make a judgment (choose a thesis) that you feel you can defend with material from the book.

Present your thesis in a standard three-part introductory paragraph—or in some subtle form of the three-part introductory paragraph. (Don't be so subtle that the thesis is not discernible). Defend and develop your thesis with two or three topic sentences that are, in turn, defended and developed with detailed information in body paragraphs.

Note: In addition to presenting and defending a judgment about the work being analyzed, a good critical review should also relate what the book (play, film, TV show, etc.) is about.

Content: The first example of assignment 7-1 uses a simple three-part introductory paragraph in which the last part previews the defense.

Jon Doe, 7-1
Eng. 122

Clemente finds the heroic in ballplayer's life

David Maraniss has long admired people who can perform on the biggest of stages. His previous biographies —of former President Bill Clinton and legendary Green Bay Packers coach Vince Lombardi—were homages to men who had what Hemingway called "grace under pressure." In *Clemente: The Passion and Grace of Baseball's Last Hero*, an account of baseball great Roberto Clemente's brilliant career as a Pittsburgh Pirate, Marannis—a *Washington Post* reporter—gives the ballplayer similar treatment. The result is an engrossing and sometimes exhilarating look at a ballplayer who was both a tremendous athlete and a fierce humanitarian.

Early in the book, Maraniss reminds the reader of just how brilliant Clemente was on the diamond from the very beginning of his career, describing the 19-year-old's "dazzling debut" in spring training after he signed with the Brooklyn Dodgers. Playing on April 1, 1954, for the Montreal Royals (a Brooklyn farm team) of the Triple-A International League, Clemente had two singles and pulled off one of the rarest feats in all of sports—an inside-the park home run. Though it would be a few seasons before Clemente started playing in the major leagues, he was clearly an up-and-coming talent. "Clemente paces Royals to win" ran the next day's headline in *The Montreal Gazette* in one of the book's

Organization: Both reviews used as examples of 7-1 use logical division as organization. Appropriate outlines would look something like this:

(first review) **Thesis**: Maraniss gives Clemente the same heroic treatment that he has given previous subjects of his biographies.

    I. Author reminds readers of Clemente's brilliance
       a. Dazzling debut
       b. Gazette headline
   II. Clemente reached heroic status in Puerto Rico
       a. '60 World Series
       b. Nightly banquets
 III. Clemente helped less fortunate
       a. Nicaragua earthquake
       b. Sportswriters' respects

(second review) **Thesis:** Book reveals how stages of life exposed Obama to many perspectives.

    I. Growing up in cosmopolitan Hawaii
       a. Met people of many races
       b. Occidental College experience
   II. Attending Harvard Law School
       a. Moved between worlds
 III. Working as community organizer in Chicago
       a. Met people of all stripes
       b. Paid off in Senate run

Note: The thesis won't always appear in the paper exactly as it is in the outline. The idea is the same, of course. Writing is, among other things, the transferring of ideas from an outline—on paper or in one's mind—into graceful prose. To do so, some changes must often be made from the way the thesis is presented in the outline. Some transitional and modifying elements may have to be added

many uses of headlines, game reports and box scores from newspapers that covered Clemente's rise and long career, which covered two decades.

As the seasons progressed and the achievements piled up, Maraniss notes, Clemente became a revered hero in his home country of Puerto Rico, where baseball is king. After the Pirates beat the New York Yankees to capture the 1960 World Series—winning the series on Bill Mazeroski's famous Game Seven homer—Clemente returned to Puerto Rico to a hero's welcome. Maraniss recreates the scene at the airport with this passage: "Handmade welcome-home placards bobbed in the milling crowd of several hundred people that awaited him on the tarmac." Maraniss also reconstructs those heady days, noting that Clemente attended nearly nightly banquets in his honor during his first month back in Puerto Rico. The future major league Hall-of-Famer received the Star Trophy as the best Latin American ballplayer and began wearing his Pirates uniform at baseball clinics he held for boys in the San Juan area.

Of course, the book also gives ample treatment to Clemente's selflessness and courage in helping the less fortunate—traits that ultimately led to his sad end. As baseball fans surely know, Clemente died when the airplane he was riding, which was full of supplies for survivors of an earthquake in Nicaragua, plunged into the Atlantic Ocean. Maraniss recounts those days after the crash when hope dwindled that Clemente would ever be found alive. The sportswriters with whom Clemente had done battle throughout his career now had the misfortune of reflecting on the ballplayer's life, rather than chronicling more games and more achievements. Phil Musick, a reso the thesis reads well with the preliminary material and with the preview of the defense—the other two elements within the introduction.

The same principle applies, of course, to other entries in the outline. The subjects and ideas remain the same, but their expression must be greatly altered to accommodate the prose presentation of these outline entries.

Shaded areas=defense:

Since a piece of writing is made up of conclusion and defense of conclusions, and since the student of writing must learn to distinguish one from the other, the sentences in these sample papers that basically present conclusions are left unshaded while the sentences that basically present defense are shaded.

Note: In the research paper, the conclusions—the thesis, division ideas, topic sentences and primary ideas plus introductory, transitional and concluding elements—are not shaded and are not documented. The defense material, on the other hand, is. The secondary and tertiary statements—sentences filled with specific detail from source material—that directly defend major conclusions are shaded and generally are documented.

porter for *The Pittsburgh Press*, recalled a shouting match he had with Clemente, as well as a moment, years later, when he felt comfortable enough to tease the slugger and got a smile in response. "When I heard that he was dead, I wished that sometime I had told him that I thought he was a hell of a guy," Musick said. "Because he was, and now it's too late to tell him there were things he did on a ballfield that made me wish I was Shakespeare."

Major League Baseball—indeed the entire professional sports world—is full of scandals, cheaters and bad behavior. In this fair and compassionate book, Maraniss shows us an athlete who invested his passion not in selfish desires but in playing a game he loved and in helping other people.

SPACING:

The spacing used for the sample themes is fairly standard and could be adopted as the required format for papers in a class, department or school. Students should note carefully any changes in the requirements listed below.

Margins: Left, right and bottom margins should be approximately one inch. The name in the name of the student should be on the first space from the top margin, followed by the name of the course and other information the instructor may request. That information should be single-spaced.

Indentation: New paragraphs should begin with a five-space indentation (type on the sixth space). Long quotes should also be indented five spaces from the left margin (type on the sixth space). New paragraphs in long quotes should be indented four more spaces—nine in from the left margin (type on the tenth space). The right hand margin for long quotes should also be indented approximately five additional spaces.

Spacing between lines: Most typed material is double spaced. In these sample papers, however, a space and a half is used so more material can be included. Students generally should double space what they type.

Jane Doe, 7-1
Eng. 122

Bridge shows encounters that shaped Obama's world view

Barack Obama's path to the White House was unlikely on many levels. As the insecure, introverted son of an African father and a white mother from Kansas, Obama didn't appear to be cut out for the world of high-level politics. Indeed, before getting his feet wet in politics by running for the Illinois state Legislature, he was mired for years in the relatively low-key jobs of community organizer and part-time teacher. All of this has been mined by newspaper reporters, and David Remnick covers similar territory in his biography of the president, *The Bridge: The Life and Rise of Barack Obama*. None of it is particularly new. What is revealing, however, is the extent to which Obama's pragmatic sensibility developed through various stages of his life, from his boyhood in Hawaii to his years as a student at Harvard Law School to his work as a community organizer in Chicago.

This broad exposure started in 1960s- and early 1970s-Hawaii, a cosmopolitan place of Indigenous islanders, whites, Japanese and blacks. It was in this racial milieu, Remnick suggests, where the future president first learned to deal with people from all walks of life—a background that suited him well when he arrived at Occidental College in California. "I think we had an immediate connection with him because we allowed him to be who he was, someone able to straddle things," Wahid Hamid, a Pakistani who was one of Obama's classmates, told Remnick. "And I think that is how Barack sees himself, as someone able to understand, for obvious reasons of his background, where both whites and blacks come from." Pondering all sides of an issue—in this case, race—started early for Obama, long before politics was at the center of his life.

That ability to straddle things continued at Harvard Law School, where Obama was chosen as president of the prestigious Harvard Law Review—in part because of his comfort level with blacks and whites, liberals and conservatives, men and women. One of his African-American classmates, Christine Spurell, told Remnick that "Barack was the one who was truly able to move between different groups and have credibility with all of them. … I don't know why at the time he was able to communicate so well with them, even spend social time with them, which was not something I would ever have done." In the end, working at the Law Review was a de-facto political experience for Obama.

Years later, after he had moved to Chicago to work as a community organizers, this exposure to people from many walks of life went even further. Remnick—the editor of *The New Yorker* magazine and the Pulitzer Prize-winning author of a book about the Soviet Union's fall—notes that life as a community organizer could be frustrating, but the tradeoff was that Obama "was getting an education: political, racial and sentimental.

He met all kinds of people he had never encountered in Hawaii or in college," such as young black nationalists, teachers, government officials, preachers, single mothers and small-business people. This all worked to Obama's advantage, Remnick shows the reader, when he ran for the state Senate in Illinois' Thirteenth District, an area whose constituents included working class folks from Chicago's gritty South Side as well as wealthy attorneys, physicians and college professors from upscale Hyde Park. Obama won election to the Legislature on his first attempt.

Three years into his presidential term, Obama and his advisers have become accustomed to both criticism and praise for his ability to seek consensus on big decisions. And it's not a small thing; indeed, perhaps his boldest piece of legislation—the national health care bill—pleased neither conservatives nor liberals because it attempted to mollify both. Remnick's book does the public a service by shedding light on how the president came to see the world in his particular way.

PART I: "WORKING PAPERS"

PROPOSALS, OUTLINES, NOTE CARDS, ETC.

Writing a research paper is a major writing assignment. As in all writing assignments, the emphasis in research paper writing should be on C and D: the **Conclusion** and **Defense** that is developed both in the introductory paragraph that reveals the thesis and in the divisions (body paragraphs) of the paper that defend the thesis.

Professional writers, on a similar project, would first use a lot of "working papers"—proposals, sketchy outlines, note cards, bibliography cards, etc. Students must start with these working papers, too.

Note on the following pages the different types of outlines students might be assigned. An outline that a student would be required to hand in would, of course, be the product of many sketchy outlines and would generally be handed in before the paper is due. Outlines are generally considered to be part of the working papers, not a part of the finished product—the paper itself. The only reflection of the outline in the paper generally is the table of contents; and, of course, the structure of the outline is reflected in the structure of the paper.

Students required to produce a research paper should find it helpful to study the assignment on the following pages and examples provided. They should be aware, however, that every assignment is different and that they need to adjust to these differences. But, basically, research paper assignments are very much like the following:

Writing Assignment 8-1

Research Paper

Write a multi-paragraph **documented subject analysis** (commonly called a research paper) of some aspect of some subject that you have **researched**. Use **any type of defense and development** that seems appropriate for your thesis. Use **any type of organization** that seems appropriate for your thesis.

Procedure: After reading widely about a subject that you are interested in, or have been assigned, formulate a tentative thesis. Take notes on material that you feel can be used in some way to defend and develop that tentative thesis.

Also, make tentative, sketchy outlines of possible ways you might defend and develop the thesis. It will help you select (and reject) material more effectively. You want to keep to a minimum the taking of notes that you will not use; yet you do not want to reject material that might help you. A tentative outline—that is changed frequently—can help determine what you need.

When you feel you have enough material to defend your tentative thesis, construct a more permanent outline—you may change it slightly before you complete the paper—that presents a logical plan for defending and developing the thesis.

Then write a rough draft of the paper. Basically, put all of the ideas from the outline—which are basically all of the major conclusions of the paper—into your own words—hopefully, graceful prose that reads well. This material will not, generally, be documented. Following each primary support idea, however, you will have to inject detailed secondary and tertiary material that will have to be documented. This specific information will be basically from your note cards and will be used in three ways: either as direct quotes, indirect quotes (paraphrases) or as summaries (précis).

Write a final draft when you feel your rough draft meets all of the requirements of acceptable writing and contains all the necessary editing.

Note: Having students fill out the form below is a good first step toward completing the analytical skeleton outline, and ultimately the full complete analytical sentence outline.

RESEARCH PAPER PROPOSAL

Tentative Topic and Thesis for Research Paper

1. What subject area are you interested in writing about?

2. What narrow aspect of the above subject area will your paper deal with?

3. What thesis (conclusion or judgment) about the aspect of your subject area do you feel you could develop into a paper?

   Subject: _____ Judgment: _____

Divisional topics (sub-theses)

4. Identify some areas (sub-theses) you feel you could develop to defend your thesis

   I. Subject: _____/

      Judgment: _____

   II. Subject: _____/

      Judgment:_____

   III. Subject: _____/

      Judgment: _____

5. What is a possible title you could use for this paper? (The title should contain the same judgment as the thesis; usually, it is a short, abbreviated version of the thesis statement appearing in the paper).

6. Why do you think such a paper is significant or worth doing?

NOTES:

NOTES:

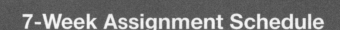
1st week: Proposal due.

2nd week: Preface due. It must be at least 150 words and one that can be used in the research paper.

3rd week: Skeleton sentence outline due. This must include the tentative thesis statement and two or more major support statements—labeled I, II, III, etc.—that reflect possible division subjects for your paper. (This is about half the complete outline)

4th week: First two paragraphs of the paper due. This must include the introductory paragraph of the paper and the introductory paragraph for the first division. The introductory paragraph, usually, contains some of the same information that appears in the preface but they are not exactly alike. The preface is usually more informal—very often containing passages in the first- or second-person (I, you, etc.). The introductory paragraph for the whole paper does not.

5th week: Sentence outline due. This must contain:

1. The thesis statement

2. Division statements: I, II, III, etc.

3. Sub-division support for at least two of I, II, III, etc. (Must have A and B under two divisions)

4. Sub-division support for at least two of A, B, C, etc. (Must have 1 and 2 under two sub-divisions)

6th week: Five works cited entries due. These must be entries of works that will be cited in the paper. Arrange alphabetically on top half of the paper.

7th week: Paper due.

The final paper should include: 1) title page, 2) preface, 3) table of contents (which should reflect the outline), 4) body of paper, 5) works cited page and 5) appendix, graphics (optional).

To be handed in with the paper: 1) a rough draft, 2) all notecards used in the paper, 3) the sentence outline that was revised by the instructor, 4) a second copy of the paper.

Remember that the paper:

(1) must include a title page, table of contents and (if required) preface.

(2) must be 8-10 pages in length (not counting the title page, table of contents and works cited page), double-spaced and written in 12-point font

(3) must use at least 7 sources—meaning at least 7 sources will appear on the works cited page

(4) must have at least 15 parenthetical citations in the body of the paper

(5) must follow format used in sample paper; for instance, there must be a main headline in upper and lowercase and in bold on the first page of the body of the paper, division headlines in upper and lowercase and in bold, and sub-headlines in upper and lower case and in bold at the beginning of paragraphs that reflect A, B, C, etc. on the outline.

(6) must include a works cited page with at least 7 entries arranged alphabetically

OUTLINES FOR RESEARCH PAPERS: A TWO-STEP APPROACH— SKELETON AND SENTENCE

The skeleton outline: This is a very basic outline that contains a tentative thesis along with statements that identify the material that will be included in each division of the paper. Note how this skeleton outline will be expanded into a fuller sentence outline that will serve as a guide for the paper.

Thesis: The most historically significant violent revolutions failed to establish viable democracies; for instance, (I) the French, (II) Chinese, (III) Russian and (IV) Cuban revolutions all failed to form democracies--as their leaders set out to do.

I. The French revolution twice established democratic governments; but one fell (A) to radicals within the movement and the other succumbed (B) to the militarist Napoleon.

II. The Chinese revolution established only a short-lived democratic order.

III. The Russian revolution at first (A) established a democracy but later (B) succumbed to the Bolsheviks.

IV. The Cuban revolution failed to establish a democratic order.

The sentence outline: This outline—an expanded version of the skeleton outline—can be very helpful in writing a research paper because the entries can very easily—with a few changes and additions—be used for the main ideas of the paper: the thesis, division topics, topic sentences and primary ideas.

Thesis: The most historically significant violent revolutions failed to establish viable democracies; for instance, (I) the French, (II) Chinese, (III) Russian and (IV) Cuban revolutions all failed to form democracies--as their leaders set out to do.

I. The French revolution twice established democratic governments; but one fell (A) to radicals within the movement and the other succumbed (B) to the militarist Napoleon.
   A. Radicals within the revolutionary movement first (1) violently ousted the elected government and, about a year later, (2) subtly took power without benefit of elections.
      1. The violent storming of the palace forced legislators to suspend the king of all duties.
      2. The subtle taking of power without elections changed the government to a dictatorship--another form of totalitarianism.
   B. The militarist Napoleon staged a coup in 1799 and France again became totalitarian.
II. The Chinese revolution established only a short-lived democratic order.
III. The Russian revolution at first (A) established a democracy but later (B) succumbed to the Bolsheviks.
   A. Establishment of democracy took place through a (1) provisional government and through (2) elections.
      1. The provisional government allowed free speech, press and dissent--the essentials of democratic order.
      2. The elections were free--with competing parties.
   B. The fall of democracy came as a result of two coups staged by the Bolsheviks: (1) one against the provisional government, (2) the other against the Constituent Assembly.
      1. The provisional government fell to the Petrograd Soviet.
      2. The Constituent Assembly was forcefully dispersed in January 1918.
IV. The Cuban revolution failed to establish a democratic order.

TAKING NOTES

Bibliography cards (note cards) should contain all of the information needed for the bibliography or works cited page entries. Whenever possible, they should also contain library call numbers for quick reference. When comments about the source are added, the bibliography cards or entries are said to be **annotated**.

Note cards must have three elements in addition to the note itself:

Source: usually author's last name or—if there is no author—part of the title; if there are several sources by one author, the source's name plus parts of a title will have to be used to identify source; a number or letter corresponding to number or letters assigned to the bibliography card can also be used to identify source.

Slug: words (or symbols)—usually placed in the upper right-hand corner of the card—that assign the material to some specific part of the paper; slug is often changed as paper is changed or reorganized.

Page number: usually placed at end of note or after the source; page number is needed in the footnote or parenthetical entry. (Often, in works from the Web, paragraph numbers are needed if no page numbers are given).

Material can be recorded on note cards in three different ways:

Direct quote: most often used (it can be changed to an indirect quote or summary, but indirect quote or summary can't easily be changed to a direct quote); be careful to have the quotation marks on the card if the note is a direct quote.

Indirect quote (paraphrase): writing material in one's own words rather than quoting directly; no enclosed in quotation marks.

Summary (précis): condensing the material before putting it on the card; not enclosed in quotation marks.

Material can be used in the paper in the same three ways that it can be recorded on cards (noted above) and must be documented—regardless of how it is used.

Some students have acquired the notion that only direct quotes need to be documented. That is not true. Indirect quotes and summaries must be documented as well as direct quotes. It is the detailed, specific information found in sources and recorded on note cards that must be documented (indicated in parenthetical citations or footnoted); the form in which the material appears in the paper—in direct quotes, indirect quotes or summaries—does not determine whether it is documented.

INTRODUCING SOURCES

When referring to a source of a quote for the first time, writers must include enough material to establish the credibility of the source. To do so, writers should provide (1) the title of the work (and the author's name, if possible); (2) the source of the work (such as a magazine or scholarly journal); (3) information about the work (and/or author) to establish it (or author) as an authority; and also (4) relate (when necessary) the work to the point being made.

First reference examples:

Further evidence of the harmful effects of having teeth x-rayed too frequently is presented by Ivan C. Marsch in his book, *Medical Tragedies*: "Dental X-ray use has ..." (105).

Even more critical of the frequent use of x-rays by dentists is an article, "Watch those X-rays," by H. Murray Callan, president of the American Dental Association. In it, he stresses, "Most dentists should not use ..." (132).

In an article on British naval operations—"The British Navy and Norway"—Harold W. Wilson, a popular Oxford professor of World War II, insists that England could have launched a successful military campaign against the Nazis in the Scandinavian countries: "The British could easily..." (43).

Harold Bold, a correspondent for the *London Times* during World War II, recently published a book, *The Norway Occupation*. In it he notes that the Nazis who occupied Oslo were "interested in using the city…" (211).

In his book, *Germany's Russian Adventure*, Mark T. Allison, Harvard's famous World War II historian, contended, "Hitler did not trust Stalin" (167).

Second reference examples (names or titles):

Allison contended, "Hitler did not trust Stalin" (167).

The article, "Hitler's Russian Move," notes, "Hitler did not trust Stalin" (53).

Wilson said the following: "Churchill did not trust his own admirals" (44).

Wilson asserts that "No German force could have…" (45).

Wilson made the following statement: "No one in the British navy…" (43).

Second reference examples (if the antecedent or reference has just been used):

He said, "Hitler did not trust Stalin" (167).

The article notes, "Hitler did not trust Stalin" (53).

To emphasize his contention that Hitler should have invaded England, he said, "He (Hitler) should not have been so cautious…" (par. 26).

The problem was made more serious, she contended, when elements…" (par. 19).

He said "absolutely no one in authority" would take charge" (78).

PART II: THE FINISHED PRODUCT

TITLE PAGE, PREFACE, TABLE OF CONTENTS, BODY, WORKS CITED PAGE (OR BIBLIOGRAPHY)

A good research paper, of course, is very much like other pieces of good writing. It has a clearly expressed thesis—often introduced with a "but" lead-in—that is defended with relevant, detailed evidence. The basic difference is that the detailed evidence in the research paper is documented (the sources are indicated in parenthetical citations, as in the sample research paper in this chapter, or footnotes).

Students should study the following sample research paper and note how it was produced from the analytical sentence outline and the note cards. This research paper is structured very rigidly—using classic introductory, body and clincher paragraphs. Standard introductory paragraphs introduce the whole paper (thesis) and the two longer divisions on France and Russia (division topics) (short papers within the long paper).

Spacing for title page: The title should be placed about two inches from the top edge and centered. The sub-title or explanation should be roughly in the middle of the paper and centered. The name of the student, the name of the instructor and information on the course, section and semester should be listed on three separate lines near the bottom, with the last line about two inches from the edge—all centered.

Preface: A preface is not always required as a part of a research paper. Your instructor may, or may not, require you to have one. Usually, it is an informal statement of purpose—what the writer intends to accomplish by writing such a paper or why he thinks such a study is significant or important.

Often a preface includes a presentation of the thesis just as the introductory paragraph of the paper itself does—usually in a different and informal way, however. Avoid using the same sentence, or sentences, to express the thesis in the preface as you do in the introductory paragraph of the research paper.

It is not unusual to use the informal first-person "I" in the preface. It is a place, too, to acknowledge special sources used or unusual help received in writing the paper.

Units of a paper labeled "Foreword," "Acknowledgements," or "Introduction" may be considered the same as a preface.

Violent Revolution:
Not the Path to Democracy

A short research paper on one aspect of several historic revolutions

By Jon Doe
Instructor Johnson
Eng122/Spring 20xx

Preface

Since this country established its democratic government through a revolution, it is popular to look with favor on all revolts by people who want freedom and independence. We tend to wish all people under totalitarian regimes would rise up in arms and set up their own free government. We encourage them to revolt and often wonder why our government does not more openly encourage rebellion in those countries which have dictators or some other form of totalitarianism.

Part of the answer probably lies in the fact that revolution has not, historically, been a very good way to move toward freedom. This paper will show that some famous revolutions have failed to achieve freedom for the masses and that promoting a revolution is a risky road to travel—that the result is not democracy, generally, but some other form of totalitarianism, often more deplorable than the one the revolution was fought to bring down.

These units, however, should never be considered the same as the first (introductory) paragraph of the paper itself—even when that first paragraph of the paper itself is labeled "introduction," as some instructors may prefer.

Table of Contents: A table of contents may, or may not, be required. Often it is not for a short research paper—such as the one used as an example in this book.

If a table of contents is used, adjustments in the above format should be made to accommodate additions to the paper—such as appendixes, glossaries and indexes.

Content and Organization: The research paper is substantially the same as all of the other papers in this book. It presents a judgment (conclusion) and defends it. Usually a long multi-paragraph paper—like the research paper—is a series of shorter papers—paragraph and short multi-paragraph themes—put together to make one longer paper.

The sample research paper above has a thesis that suggests four divisions. Consequently, there are four short papers put together into one larger paper. Two of the shorter papers (divisions)—on China and Cuba—are one-paragraph themes; two—on France and Russia—are short multi-paragraph themes—each with its own introductory paragraph, body paragraphs and concluding paragraph.

Introductory paragraph: The sample paper above begins with a simple three-part introductory paragraph that introduces the whole paper. The first two sentences contain **preliminary, "lead-in" material**; the third and fourth sentences present the thesis; and the last three sentences contain **a preview of the defense and development**. In this preview, there is an allusion to four revolutions that failed to produce lasting

Establishing and defending such a premise should serve to make our government's reluctance to openly back rebellion seem more reasonable. It may explain, too, why our government often tolerates totalitarian governments—like Spain, Greece and others. Cautiously encouraging these governments to evolve slowly towards democracy perhaps makes more sense than encouraging the people in those countries to revolt, especially since—as this paper will show—famous revolts in the past have failed to establish democratic political orders—even when they were fought primarily to do so.

Table of Contents

Violent Revolution – Not the Path to Democracy

Because the United States established its democratic government following a violent revolution, it has been popular to think that armed rebellion is the best way for an oppressed people to acquire freedom. It is not unusual for free people to encourage those living under totalitarian governments to revolt—violently, if necessary—and establish a democratic political order in the wake of the revolution.

democracies. How they failed, of course, will be more fully explained in the paper. These explanations will serve as the basic defense and development of the thesis and will, logically enough, be presented in four divisions.

First division: The second paragraph is another standard introductory paragraph. The first two sentences contain the **preliminary**, "**lead in**" **material** that makes a smooth transition—primarily through repetition of key words—to the division topic (the "thesis" of the division). It will have two parts—one on extremists, one on a military coup. The third sentence presents the **division topic**. The last sentence contains **a preview of the defense and development** of the division.

The third paragraph is really the first body paragraph of the first division. It will develop fully the part extremists had in frustrating the revolution and it will, of course, contain some documented material.

Note: The first division is very simple structurally. It is a four-paragraph paper with short introductory and concluding paragraphs and two longer body paragraphs.

Documenting: Generally, about one half of the paper is documented; about one half is not.

Remember that conclusions are not documented. That means that in any research paper the major conclusions—sentences and phrases that contain the **thesis, division topics, topic sentences** and **primary support ideas**—are not documented. It further means that elements—minor conclusions—which basically make **introductions** (to a whole paper, to a division within a paper or to a paragraph), which make **transitions** (between paragraphs or within paragraphs)

Unfortunately, very few revolutions have led to lasting democratic political orders. In fact, the most histrocially significant revolutions failed to establish viable democracies—even though they were fought in the name of freedom and self-government. The violent French Revolution in 1789, the Chinese in 1911, the Russian in 1917, and the Cuban in 1959—none of these famous bloody revolts produced strong, lasting democracies, even though their leaders proclaimed that was their goal. Three of these revolutions—the French, the Chinese and the Russian—did produce shaky democracies, but these governments succumbed quickly and easily to totalitarian forces that took over by force and established new non-democratic governments. The Cuban revolution has yet to produce free elections or any of the other basic freedoms considered essential for a democratic political order.

France's Democracy Falls Twice

The French Revolution in 1789, perhaps the most significant historically, failed to establish a strong democratic political order that could survive. Under the banner of Liberty, Equality and Fraternity, the French revolutionaries twice set up governments that—for that time in history, at least—were quite democratic. These representative governing bodies, however, did not last long. One was disrupted and eventually replaced by revolutionary extremists; the other was disbanded by a military coup.

Radicals take over: The first constitutional representative government succumbed to radicals within the revolutionary movement. The first attack on the elected legislators came when

or which make **concluding statements** (clincher statements, summaries) are not documented.

The secondary and tertiary statements, however, must be documented when they contain detailed information from some source. In most research papers, the detailed information used for defense and development comes from some printed source—not from the writer's imagination, observation, general knowledge or wide reading—and must be documented.

Note: Anyone who does extensive research on some subject can recall some details, and when these are used in the paper, they need not be documented. In the sample research paper, for instance, the writer cites, in the introductory paragraph, the specific years for the various revolutions. No doubt, in doing research for the paper, he had read about those dates so often they became for him general knowledge about the subject and he did not have to refer to notes or sources when he needed to use them in the paper.

A safe guide would be this: if you have to check your notes or some source to verify the details, you should document; if you can recall the information without referring to notes or sources and if it is of such a general nature that anyone who had read widely on the subject could recall it without referring to notes or sources, then you do not have to document the material. In this paper—or in any other research paper, for that matter—the first (introductory) paragraph does not generally contain documented material. It usually contains preliminary material, a thesis and a preview of the defense—none of which needs to be documented.

The second paragraph in the sample paper is an introductory paragraph, too (it introduces the first division), and has nothing in it that needs to be documented.

some of the leaders of the revolution insisted that the king be stripped of the powers he had been granted under the new government—a constitutional monarchy. One account of the insurrection, in a volume entitled *The Record of Mankind*, related that "On August 10, 1792, a mob stormed the Tuileries [the palace], massacred the Swiss Guard, and forced the Legislative Assembly to suspend the king from his duties until his fate could be decided" (Roehm 311). About a year later, these extremists subtly took power and France found itself once again under a totalitarian regime. One historian, Louis L. Snyder, in writing of the take-over, notes that:

> In the spring of 1793 the National Convention entrusted supreme executive authority to a Committee of Public Safety composed originally of nine and later of twelve members. This small body included such Jacobin leaders as Danton, Robspierre, Saint-Just, and Carnot. At first the members were to hold office for only a month, but soon they continued on without the formality of elections. Transformed almost imperceptibly into dictatorship, the Committee directed military operations, administered finance, appointed and dismissed ministers and suppressed all criticism. (231)

Another historian, Arthur J. May —in his two volume work, *A History of Civilization* - called these radicals who took over France by force totalitarians and wrote of their ruthless tactics:

In the third paragraph—the first body paragraph of the first division—one can expect some secondary, and possibly some tertiary, support material that needs to be documented. It would not ordinarily be in the first sentence; that is generally the topic sentence—a major conclusion; nor would it usually appear in the second sentence; that is generally a primary support idea—another major conclusion. But, in the third sentence of the paragraph, one usually finds specific information that needs to be documented.

Note: Often a sentence is partly a primary idea (generalization) that should not be documented and partly a secondary statement that should be documented. In such a case, document the whole sentence or at least the part that needs to be.

Notice how in most body paragraphs throughout the paper, there are are transitional sentences—not documented, of course—that basically separate parts of the paragraph that are documented. These transitional sentences generally contain a new primary support idea as well—another reason for their not being documented.

Material can be used in the paper in the same three ways that it can be recorded on cards (noted above) and must be documented—regardless of how it is used.

Some students have acquired the notion that only direct quotes need to be documented. That is not true. Indirect quotes and summaries must be documented as well as direct quotes. It is the detailed, specific information found in sources and recorded on note cards that must be documented; the form in which the material appears in the paper—in direct quotes, indirect quotes or sumaries—does not determine whether it is documented.

Second division: The second division—an allusion to China's revolution—is very short: a one-paragraph theme. Notice the transitional word

For fourteen months France was ruled by a ruthless and relentless oligarchy of Jacobins, organized as a Committee of Public Safety … The Committee resorted to dread terror in order to frighten domestic opponents into submission or to erase them forever.

In Paris the instrument of Jacobin terrorism was a notorious revolutionary tribunal, which summarily tried and summarily guillotined individuals who were openly at odds with the Jacobin junta or who were suspected of disloyalty … They slaughtered and slew without mercy; in Lyons, as an example, about 4,000 were killed in mass butcheries. Ruthless terror coerced France into submission to the Jacobin dictatorship. (225)

France's first attempt to establish a democratic political order had failed miserably—primarily because of dissidents within the revolutionary movement itself who wrested power illegally from the elected, legally constituted government.

Napoleon's coup: The second representative French government, established by the revolutionists after the "Reign of Terror," fell, after only a few years, to the famous militarist Napoleon Bonaparte. Snyder, in his account of the Coup d' etat, states that Bonaparte deliberately planned the overthrow. "Napoleon's hour had come," he writes. "Weary of war, [the French people] longed for a strong hand who could put an end to perpetual conflict aboard and anarchic conditions at home … Napoleon

"Another" that helps make a smooth transition to the new division and also helps show that the new division has the same relationship to the thesis that the first division has. (Transitional words help show how new material relates to the major conclusion being defended).

Third division: The third division—on Russia's revolution—is a longer multi-paragraph paper. It begins with a subtle variation of the standard introductory paragraph. The first sentence contains **preliminary**, **"lead in"** material that serves as transition—again primarily through repetition of key words. The second and third sentences present both the division topic—that Russia's revolution failed in its mission—and a preview of the defense and development.

Note: The defense and development in the third division will be presented in a type of organization that is **logical order** rather than **logical division**. It will defend the division idea by first establishing that a democracy did indeed exist and then by showing that it succumbed to coup and thus failed. These are not two equal parts—two paragraphs having the same relationship to the division idea—as one would need to use logical division.

The third division does not have the conventional short concluding paragraph. Rather, the writer chose to establish that the communists who came to power were not democratic. By doing so, the writer further defends his division idea—that the revolution failed to establish a democracy as it had intended.

Numbering of pages (pagination): The usual practice for student papers is as follows:

All pages up to the first page of the body of the paper are numbered with small Roman numerals—the title page,

surveyed the situation and decided to organize a conspiracy to overthrow the directory" (Snyder 335). May—in his rather colorful account of the takeover—says,

> Soldiers in Paris were placed under command of the popular and picturesque General, who presently summoned the legislature to turn power over to him. When the lawmakers indignantly balked, Bonaparte staged a military putsch, in November, 1799, ordering troops to disperse the dissenters. A rump legislature then did the general's bidding. Another constitution was drafted assigning the executive authority to a First consul, Bonaparte, and two subordinate consuls; an imposing array of legislative bodies was created but they were purely ornamental and decorative. (231)

In writing about Napoleon's seizure of power, the authors of *The Record of Mankind* quote the famous general saying, "I found the crown of France lying on the ground and I picked it up with a sword" (Roehm 316).

The French Revolution, then, failed to produce the new democratic political order that the American Revolution had—really the goal of its most ardent leaders. As a preface to his chapter on the French Revolution, Snyder uses a brief article by one Leo Gershoy. Towards the end of the essay, Gershoy makes this pertinent statement: "In 1799 when Bonaparte seized power, the Revolution had sorely dissapointed the expectations of

table of contents, preface, etc.—in the upper righthand corner. All pages in the rest of the paper (except the works cited page) are numbered with Arabic numerals—in the upper righthand corner.

An alternative style is this:

Do not number the title page, table of contents, preface or first page of the body of the paper; rather, begin numbering with the Arabic numeral 2 on the second page and number the rest of the pages (but not the works cited page)—all in the upper righthand corner. Follow your instructor's directions.

Shaded areas=defense: Since a piece of writing is made up of conclusion and defense of conclusions, and since the student of writing must learn to distinguish one from the other, the sentences in these sample papers that basically present conclusions are left unshaded while the sentences that basically present defense are shaded.

Note: In the research paper, the **conclusions**—the thesis, division ideas, topic sentences and primary ideas plus introductory, transitional and concluding elements—are **not shaded** and are **not documented**. The **defense** material, on the other hand, is. The **secondary and tertiary statements**—sentences filled with specific detail from source material—that directly defend major conclusions **are shaded** and generally **are documented**.

Spacing: The spacing used for the sample themes is fairly standard and could be adopted as the required format for papers in a class, department or school. Students should note carefully any changes in the requirements listed below.

Margins: Left, right, top and bottom margins should be approximately one inch.

the many followers" (qtd. in Snyder 231). After 1799, many more followers of revolutionary movements were to be "sorely dissapointed." The revolts—especially the violent revolts—that many fought so hard to bring about did not very often produce the strong democracies that the revolutionaries most often sought to establish.

China's Democracy Did Not Last

Another historically significant revolution that dissapointed its leaders was the Chinese revolt of 1911. May relates that the revolution at first succeeded in establishing a democratic political order. "The detested Manchu autocracy," he noted, "was cast into discord and a democratic republic was installed in its stead" (517). But the democracy was short-lived. The account of the revolution in *The Record of Mankind* has the following passages that explain in part why the representative government failed:

> The Revolution of 1911-1912 freed China from rule by the Manchus, but not from the curse of civil strife. Ever since the imperial government fell, China has been kept in turmoil, because of the greed for power and plunder on the part of military leaders and governors, the activities of the Communists, and the raids of bandits. Dr. Sun Yat-sen, the revered leader of the revolution, governed only the south of China. When he died in 1925 his party (the Kuomintang) contained two factions. One group wished to improve the condition of the masses;

WRITING INSIGHTS: Discovering the Keys to Structure and Content

Indentation: New paragraphs should begin with a five-space indentation (type on the sixth space). Long quotes should also be indented five spaces from the left margin (type on the sixth space). New paragraphs in long quotes should be indented four more spaces—nine in from the left margin (type on the tenth space). The right hand margin for long quotes should also be indented approximately five additional spaces.

Fourth division: The last division—on Cuba's revolution—is also very short—a one-paragraph theme. Notice the use of both the transitional word "also" and the repetition of key words and word groups (like "revolution" and "failed to create a democracy") to move effectively into the last division of defense and development.

The concluding (clincher) paragraph: The final paragraph makes a fairly standard concluding statement. Like most closing paragraphs, it contains basically the same elements that an introductory paragraph has: **preliminary information**, **a thesis** and **a preview of the defense**. The first sentence has the preliminary, "lead in" information that serves both to introduce the concluding statement and to make a transition from the last division to the closing comments.

The second sentence repeats the idea expressed in the thesis. The third sentence is a short digression that makes a slight concession to the idea that revolutions have helped nations move toward democracy. But the next sentence immediately returns to the thesis through restatement. The last two sentences contain additional information about the four areas of defense—not only to review the major defense and development conclusions used in the paper, as a good concluding paragraph often does, but also **to emphasize** the major areas of defense used in the paper.

---

it contained a number of Communists. The other group believed that the first need of China was a strong central government which could unite the country. Chiang Kai-shek led the second group. He won control of southern China, then conqured most of the north, and made himself virtual dictator. (Roehm 624)

In his concluding statement on China's revolutionary years, Snyder wrote, "China had suffered decades of terrible civil war and apparently was still unready for free democratic government on the Western model" (511). Chiang Kai-shek ultimately was ousted from China, in 1949, and power went to another anti-democratic force—the Communist party. China is still without the democracy the leaders of its revolution sought.

Russia's Democracy Short-Lived

Almost as important historically as the French Revolution was the Russian revolt against the Czars in 1917. It, too, was fought primarily to establish a democratic political order. It, too, failed to reach its goal.

Democracy established: Since the Communists came to power after the Russian Revolution, it seems reasonable to assume that a communist government was the goal of the revolution. It was not. Historians invariably write about the democracy the revolutionaries established and tried to maintain. Part of May's account of the revolution bears the headline, "A Democratic Interlude." Under it, he writes:

Works cited/bibliography: The works cited page for the sample research paper contains only those sources that were documented (cited) in the paper.

Some bibliographies, on the other hand, contain more than the sources documented in the text. Sometimes (as in papers that use traditional footnoting), they also include sources in which the writer did wide reading about her topic but from which she did not draw specific information that needed to be documented.

Bibliographies often contain, too, lists of sources relevant to the topic that the writer has not read, but that she feels might be helpful to some reader who might want to study the subject. If your instructor permits you to include more than the sources cited, be careful to include only those relevant to your subject and thesis.

For eight months, until the Bolshevik seizure of power, public authority was lodged in a Provisional Government made up of Duma men; it was republican, and the most democratic regime Russia had ever experienced.

Freedom of press and speech and other civil liberties were proclaimed, political prisoners amnestied, and minorities were assured the right of self-determination. To prepare a constitution, an assembly would be chosen by universal adult suffrage. (612)

In writing about the provisional government, the authors of *The Record of Mankind* include this statement: "It seemed to the outside world that Russia was on the road to liberal democracy" (Roehm 586). Late in 1917—ironically after the Bolshevik coup—Russia even had a free election. Approximately 36,000,000 people voted and elected representatives to the Constituent Assembly—a body that was to prepare a constitution. About 9,000,000 voted for Bolshevik deputies; 21,000,000 voted for Alexander Kerensky's party—which was heading the democratic provisional government—and 6,000,000 voted for less powerful factions (Palmer and Colton 615). Of the election, May wrote, "that was the only opportunity Russia ever had of expressing itself freely in a democratic election with competing parties and universal, direct and secret voting" (615).

Bolshevik coups: Despite the apparent desire of the Russian people to maintain a democratic political order, the revolution failed to do so. It succumbed instead to the Bolsheviks, a well-organized minority party that seized power by force and set up a very undemocratic government—totalitarian and in many respects similar to the oppressive regime of the Czars which it replaced. Two historians, R.R. Palmer and Joel Colton—in their book, *A History of the Modern World*—give this account of the coup by the Bolsheviks:

> Lenin now judged that the hour had come for the seizure of power . . . On the night of November 6-7, 1917, the Bolsheviks took over telephone exchanges, railway stations, and electric lighting plants in the city. A warship turned its guns on the Winter Palace, where Kerensky's government sat. The latter could find almost no one to defend it. The hastily assembled congress of soviets pronounced the Provisional Government defunct, and named in its place a "council of people's commissars," of which Lenin became the head. (723-724)

Another account of the coup, in *The Record of Mankind*, stated simply that "the Petrograd Soviet led a second revolution which easily overthrew the Kerensky government" (Roehm 587). The Bolsheviks also forcefully broke up the constitutional assembly that was elected in Russia's only free election—noted previously in this paper. The elections, curiously enough, were held after the November seventh coup. They had been promised to the people by the provisional government. The Bolsheviks allowed them to be held, then forced the assembly to disband. May notes that the elections were held but that the Bolsheviks lost so they staged a second coup (615). The account of the Constituent Assembly in a *History of the Modern World* states that "The Assembly was broken up on the second day of its session; armed sailors dispatched by the people's commissars simply surrounded it (Palmer and Colton 724).

The Bolsheviks who came to power were basically anti-democracy and, of course, did not establish a democratic political order—the goal of the revolution. One source made this statement about the consequences of the Bolshevik ouster of the elected constitutional assembly:

> The dissolution of the Constituent Assembly was a frank repudiation of majority rule in favor of "class rule"—to be exercised for the proletariat by the Bolsheviks. The dictatorship of the proletariat was now established. Two months later, in March 1918, the Bolsheviks renamed themselves the Communist Party. (Palmer and Colton 724)

The same source quoted Lenin as saying, "to hand over power to the Constituent Assembly would again be compromising with the malignant bourgeoisie" (Palmer and Colton 724). Excerpts from May's coverage of the Bolsheviks state clearly that the government established by the Communists was not democratic but totalitarian:

Avowedly it was a dictatorship of the proletariat, but in reality it was a dictatorship imposed upon the proletariat and everyone else—and that by revolutionaries ostensibly dedicated to the loftiest aspirations of mankind (614).

Whatever the theory, whatever the blueprint for the future, the Soviet government in day-to-day action and performance was strictly authoritarian and totalitarian...

Constitutionalism in Soviet Russia has never been other than window dressing. All public questions began—and begin—with the Communist Party. Proudly hailed as the militant vanguard, the party contained (1939) just under 2,500,000, counting candidates, or possibly 4 percent of the adult population. (614)

Life magazine, in a recent article on revolution, made the following pertinent statement about democracy and Lenin, the leader of the Communist regime that came to power during the Russian Revolution:

Though he believed in democracy—or said he did—Lenin thought the proletariat would never win without a dedicated elite to lead them; the Bolshevik party was the precision instrument that swept him to power in a lightning coup against a shaky 8-month-old government. But because of Lenin's faith in an elite, his one original thought to the revolutionary theory, the proletariat was in the end betrayed. The party reaped the fruits of the revolution, and as it slowly stiffened into a crushing bureaucracy, the masses sank back into an impotence as profound as under the Czars. ("Revolution" 110-111)

Another revolution had failed to produce a democracy—the kind of government its leaders had so desperately tried to establish.

Cuba's Democracy Did Not Emerge

The most sensational recent revolution—Castro's rise to power in Cuba—also failed to create a democracy, as the revolutionary leaders there—including Castro, ironically—advocated. Before he came to power, Castro promised he would establish a democratic political order. In his speeches and written pronouncements, he said he would restore to the people of Cuba the rights guaranteed under the 1940 Constitution—including free elections, free press and free speech ("Cuba" 288e-288f). "Power does not interest me and I will not take it, Castro insisted after his 26th of July Movement had ousted the dictator Batista. "From now on," he proclaimed, "the people are entirely free" ("Cuba—End of War" 34). Cubans expected a democracy. But Castro, surprisingly, soon established a very non-democratic government: a modern totalitarian political order—communism. Shortly after coming to power, he declared that constitutional government—with free, democratic elections—would not be possible for four or five years ("Cuba" 288f). Late in 1961, on December 21, Castro declared: "I am a Marxist-Leninist to the last day of my life" (Monahan and Gilmore 184). Cuba has since been governed by a one-party, dictatorial political order similar to those of the communist bloc nations ("Cuba" 280). The only political party allowed is the Cuban Communist Party (PCC), which is governed by a one hundred-man central committee, an eight-man Politburo and a six-man Secretariat ("Cuba" 288h). Another revolution failed in its mission—the creation of a democracy.

Violent revolutions, then—ever since the American Revolution—have been fought primarily to establish democratic governments that allow citizens a great measure of personal and political freedom—especially free elections, free press and free speech. Almost invariably, however, these violent revolts have failed in their mission. It is true, of course, that they have often helped move nations toward more democratic political orders. In most of them, however, the movement has been almost imperceptible. Of the countries cited in this paper, only France, ultimately—about 50 years after its revolution began—established a representative government. The other three—China, Russia and Cuba—still have not moved from totalitarianism—the very kind of government their people revolted against—to a democratic order of some kind—the type of government their revolutionary leaders seemed so desperately to be seeking.

Works Cited

"Cuba." *Encyclopedia Americana.* International ed. 1968: 278-288h. Print.

"Cuba—End of War." *Time* 12 Oct. 1959: 33-35. Print.

May, Arthur J. *A History of Civilization*, 2nd ed., II. New York: Charles Scribner's Sons, 1964.

Monahan, James, and Kenneth O. Gilmore. *The Great Deception*. New York: Farrar, Strauss Company, 1963.

Palmer, R.R., and Joel Colton. *A History of the Modern World*, 3rd ed. New York: Alfred A. Knopf, 1965.

"Revolution." *Life* 10 Oct. 1969: 101-112. Print.

Roehm, Wesley A., and others. *The Record of Mankind*. Boston: D.C. Health and Company, 1956.

Snyder, Lois L. *The Making of Modern Man*. Princeton, New Jersey: D. Van Nostrand Company, Inc., 1967. Print.

CITING SOURCES IN THE TEXT

In research paper writing, much of the material that students use in the defense of their theses must be cited. While footnoting has long been one method of citation used in composition courses, contemporary students often cite sources according to styles created by the Modern Language Association (MLA) and the American Psychological Association (APA). MLA style is popular, generally, for humanities courses while APA style is often used for papers dealing with the sciences.

Under MLA formatting, citations in the text of papers include the last name of the author and the page number of the source (Anderson 47). [Note that no comma is used between the name and page number]. If the author is unknown, a version of the title of the source and a page number is given; if the source is accessed on the Web and a page number is not provided, often the paragraph number is used in the citation.

According to APA style, meanwhile, citations in the text of papers include the last name of the author and the date the source was published (Anderson, 2014). [Note the comma between the author and date]. Students quoting the source must also include a page number after the date, when possible (Anderson, 2014, p. 47). [Note the comma between the date and the page number].

These are general guidelines, of course, and may not apply in the case of every source that needs to be documented. For further information, refer to Modern Language Association Web site (www.mla.org) or the American Psychological Association Web site (www.apa.org).

CREATING A WORKS CITED PAGE

Besides in-text citations (citations in the body of the paper), both MLA and APA styles include matching bibliographic entries at the end of the paper. Here are some examples of bibliographic or works cited entries in both styles. The list is not exhaustive.

MLA style:
Traditional sources:
Book, one author:

Remnick, David. *The Bridge: The Life and Rise of Barack Obama*. New York: Alfred A. Knopf, 2010.
    Print.

Book, two or three authors:

Bernstein, Carl, and Bob Woodward. *All the President's Men*. New York: Simon and Schuster,
    1974. Print.

Unknown or anonymous author:

Primary Colors. New York: Random House, 1996. Print.

Book with an author and an editor:

Aamot, Paul. *Writing Insights: Discovering the Keys to Structure and Content.* Ed. Gregg Aamot. Dubuque, IA: Kendall Hunt Publishing Co., 2014. Print.

Encyclopedia or dictionary entry:

"Harry S. Truman." *The Encyclopedia Americana.* 2004 ed. Print.

Web sources:

Article in a newspaper:

Neal, La Velle E. III. "Mauer Takes Grounders at First." *Star Tribune.* Star Tribune, 28 June 2011. Web. 24 Apr. 2014.

Article in a weekly or biweekly magazine:

Remnick, David. "We Are Alive." *New Yorker.* New Yorker, 30 July 2012. Web. 24 Apr. 2014.

Article in a monthly or bimonthly magazine:

Rosenberg, Tina. "The Underdogs' Guru." *Atlantic Monthly.* Atlantic Monthly, Oct. 2013. Web. 24 Apr. 2014.

Article in a scholarly journal:

Covassin, Tracey, R.J. Elbin, and Kelly Sarmiento. "Educating Coaches About Concussion In Sports: Evaluation Of The CDC's 'Heads Up: Concussion In Youth Sports' Initiative." *Journal Of School Health,* Journal Of School Health, May 2012. Web. 24 Apr. 2014.

Newspaper Op/Ed piece:

Friedman, Thomas L. "My President is Busy." *New York Times.* New York Times, 11 Nov. 2012. Web. 24 Apr. 2014.

Newspaper editorial, unsigned:

"Welcome to the U, Former Secretary Rice." *Star Tribune.* Star Tribune, 17 Apr. 2014. Web. 24 Apr. 2014.

Web site:

National Council of Teachers of English. Home page. Apr. 2014. Web. 26 Apr. 2014.

Document from a Web site:

"FDA to regulate e-cigarettes, additional tobacco products." American Medical Association. 24 Apr. 2014. Web. 29 Apr. 2014.

E-book:

Brown, Curt. *In the Footsteps of Little Crow: 150 Years After the U.S.-Dakota War*. Minneapolis: Star Tribune Media Co., 2013. *Startribune.com*. Web. 29 Apr. 2014.

APA style:
Traditional sources:
Book, one author:

Remnick, D. (2010). *The Bridge: The Life and Rise of Barack Obama*. New York: Alfred A. Knopf.

Book, two or three authors:

Bernstein, C., & Woodward, B. (1974). *All the President's Men*. New York: Simon and Schuster.

Unknown or anonymous author:

Primary Colors. (1996). New York: Random House.

Book with an author and an editor:

Aamot, P. (2014). *Writing Insights: Discovering the Keys to Structure and Content* (G. Aamot, Ed.). Dubuque, IA: Kendall Hunt Publishing Co.

Encyclopedia or dictionary entry:

"Harry S. Truman." (2004). *The Encyclopedia Americana*.

Web sources:

Article in a newspaper:

Neal, L. E., III (2011, June 28). Mauer Takes Grounders at First. *Star Tribune*. Retrieved May 11, 2014, from http://www.startribune.com

Article in a weekly or biweekly magazine:

Remnick, D. (2012, July 30). We Are Alive. *New Yorker*. Retrieved May 11, 2014, from http://www.newyorker.com

Article in a monthly or bimonthly magazine:

Rosenberg, T. (2013, October). The Underdog's Guru. Retrieved Jan. 1, 2014, from
http://www.theatlantic.com

Article in a scholarly journal with DOI assigned:

Covassin, T., Elbin, R. J., & Sarmiento, K. (2012). Educating Coaches About Concussion in
Sports: Evaluation of the CDC's 'Heads Up: Concussion in Youth Sports' Initiative.
Journal Of School Health, *82*(5), 233-238. doi:10.1111/j.1746-1561.2012.00692.x

Newspaper Op/Ed piece:

Friedman, T. L. (2012, Nov 11). My president is busy. *New York Times*. Retrieved June 13,
2013, from http://www.nytimes.com

Newspaper editorial, unsigned:

Welcome to the U, former Secretary Rice. (2014, Apr 17). *Star Tribune*. Retrieved April 28, 2014,
from http://www.startribune.com

Web site:

National Council of Teachers of English. (2014, Apr.). Home page. Apr. 2014.

E-book:

Brown, C. (2014). *In the Footsteps of Little Crow.* Retrieved April 29, 2014, from
http://www.startribune.com

Critical Thinking

WHAT IS LOGIC?

Simply stated, logic is the process (thinking, reasoning) by which man makes decisions—hopefully valid (reasonable) conclusions (judgments) about what he perceives. Another way to state it: logic is used in conclusion- (judgment) making. Ask a person what he thinks about a subject, and she replies with what she has concluded about the subject—her decision or judgment about the topic.

LOGIC AND WRITING

Writers present conclusions—decisions, judgments, solutions to problems—in what they write. They use logic to formulate these conclusions. They present them in theses, in division topics, in topic sentences and primary ideas within paragraphs.

People are not always skillful conclusion-makers. They are often biased, prejudiced, irrational, unfair, unprincipled, self-serving, etc. But as writers people must try to present conclusions that are rational, logical, acceptable. Consequently, students of writing must study logical fallacies—errors that can be made in logic (thinking) and reflected in writing.

There are many terms and phrases commonly used to respond to or evaluate people's conclusion- (judgment, decision) making capacity that might help to give students more insight into what logic is all about. Some are listed below:

Synonyms for good, sound logic	**Synonyms for poor, faulty logic:**
1. logical	1. illogical
2. reasonable	2. unreasonable
3. sensible (common sense)	3. nonsense
4. makes sense	4. doesn't make sense
5. rational	5. irrational
6. good judgment	6. poor judgment
7. thinking straight	7. faulty thinking
8. using your head	8. not using your head
9. putting two and two together	9. doesn't add up
10. making logical deductions	10. doesn't follow
11. logical conclusions	11. logical fallacies

Note: The study of logic traditionally deals with various types of errors in logic (logical fallacies) which are identified with various terms—many of them Latin, because the study of logic has been going on for a long time. It's an old subject.

HOW DOES MAN THINK (MAKE CONCLUSIONS)?

Logicians and scholars of logic have always contended that man makes conclusions (thinks) in only two basic ways: inductively and deductively. He often makes conclusions (decisions) based on evidence (inductive reasoning), and he also often makes conclusions based on other conclusions that he has come to accept (deductive reasoning).

The diagram below is one graphic way by which the two thinking processes are shown in some texts on logic:

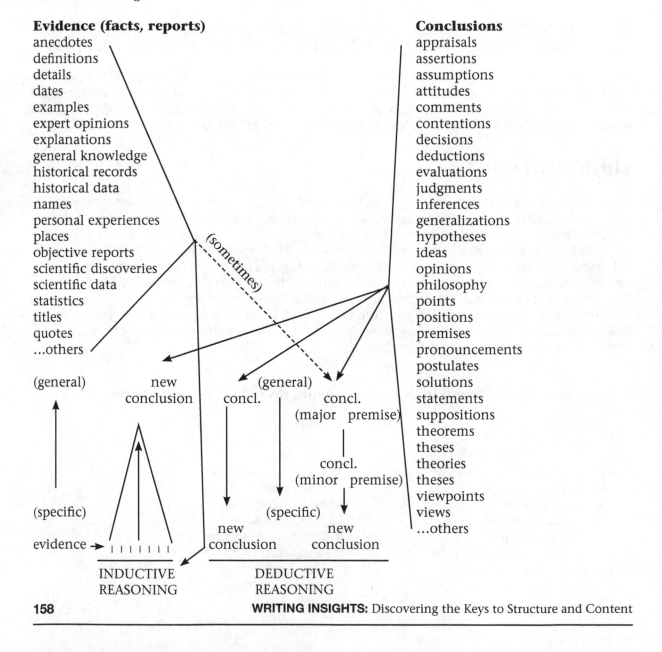

Evidence (facts, reports)

anecdotes
definitions
details
dates
examples
expert opinions
explanations
general knowledge
historical records
historical data
names
personal experiences
places
objective reports
scientific discoveries
scientific data
statistics
titles
quotes
...others

Conclusions

appraisals
assertions
assumptions
attitudes
comments
contentions
decisions
deductions
evaluations
judgments
inferences
generalizations
hypotheses
ideas
opinions
philosophy
points
positions
premises
pronouncements
postulates
solutions
statements
suppositions
theorems
theses
theories
theses
viewpoints
views
...others

(sometimes)

(general)   new conclusion   (general) concl.   concl. (major premise)

concl. (minor premise)

(specific)   (specific)

evidence → | | | | | | | new conclusion   new conclusion

INDUCTIVE REASONING   DEDUCTIVE REASONING

Note: Deductive reasoning structures that use major and minor premises are called syllogisms. Syllogisms in which either the major premise, minor premise or the new conclusion is implied are called enthymemes.

Enthymeme	**Syllogism**
Look out for that car!	**Major premise:** All student drivers are dangerous
There's a student driver!	**Minor premise:** That driver is a student
	New conclusion: That driver is dangerous

Note: A person who would say "Look out for that car! There's a student driver!" probably would object if someone said to him or her "So, you think all student drivers are dangerous!" But that is the major premise implied. The new conclusion, "That driver is dangerous," is also implied in the enthymeme.

The new conclusion is not acceptable because most people would not logically accept the Major Premise. The syllogism's pattern is acceptable, but the syllogism is considered faulty because the Major Premise is faulty.

Enthymeme	**Syllogism**
Well, if George is in college,	**MP:** All college students are high school graduates
he must be a high school graduate	**mp:** George is in college
	NC: George is a high school graduate

Note: Again, the new conclusion may be wrong because the Major Premise is wrong.

Enthymeme	**Syllogism**
If nation X is a democracy, it has	**MP:** All democracies have a free pass
a free press	**mp:** Nation X is a democracy
	NC: Nation X has a free press

Note: New conclusion is acceptable if the major and minor premises are accepted as true.

Note: Scholars of logic say there are a hundred or so acceptable patterns and variations of syllogisms. Most important, however, is that the major and minor premises must be accepted as logical before the new conclusion can be accepted.

People rarely use the word premise in conversation, speeches and writing. They generally use one of the 25 or so synonyms for conclusion cited on previous pages: **I think** that…(most common); **I believe** that…, **I feel** that…, **I agree** that…, **I propose** that…, **It is my position** that…, I accept the following **hypothesis**, or **theory**, or **thesis**, or **view**, etc.

The diagram here tries to show that some synonyms for conclusions tend to be used when the decision is objective, others when it is highly subjective and still others when it is basically neutral. The position of each term on the continuum, of course, is highly debatable.

Objective:

Unbiased, free of personal prejudice, emotion, surmise. Many writers, especially journalists, prize objectivity.

Outside one's self. Usually thought of as positive.

Although writers seek to be objective, complete objectivity in writing, according to most journalism experts, is in most instances impossible.

Subjective:

Often biased, prejudiced, emotional, opinionated.
Self is involved.

Usually thought of as negative. However, much of the great literature is very subjective.

Subjective analysis of news events by learned writers and reporters is more valued now than it was in decade past.

Good readers detect the bias in all that they read, according to experts in reading. And all bias is not bad.

Note: Perhaps there are many synonyms for the product of man's thinking—the conclusions, the judgments, the decisions he makes—because he finds a need to cover up the subjective nature of much of his decision making. Some of the diversity of terms, however, is understandable. He needs to distinguish between decisions that are arrived at quickly and without much study—which he calls **opinions**, **judgments**, etc.—and those that are arrived at very carefully and scientifically after much study and research—which he tends to label **theorems**, **theories**, etc. Sometimes, however, he euphemistically uses terms like **postulates**, **hypothesis** and **premises** for mere snap judgments and opinions.

objective
- theorems
- hypotheses
- postulates
- theories
- philosophies
- premises
- theses
- deductions
- inferences
- assumptions

neutral
- statements
- ideas
- comments
- generalizations
- points

subjective

viewpoints	attitudes
views	decisions
solutions	evaluations
assertions	position
assessments	suppositions
appraisals	judgments
contentions	opinions
beliefs	

Printed in the USA
CPSIA information can be obtained
at www.ICGtesting.com
JSHW060207251123
52571JS00003B/4